# How to Develop the I Outstanding Teaching

There can arguably be no greater influence on a person's life than their education, and it is the classroom practice of teachers that helps to shape young lives. *How to Develop the Habits of Outstanding Teaching* aims to help teachers improve their teaching habits and practice so that every student can be supported, challenged and inspired to achieve their ambitions and goals.

Providing a step-by-step guide to the key components for creating outstanding lessons, the book includes a wealth of strategies and techniques that are easy to implement and will have an immediate impact on your teaching and students. With a wide range of examples and case studies taken from different subjects, the book covers all aspects of teaching, including:

- how to create independence, resilience and creativity;

- tried-and-tested techniques for differentiation and questioning;

- habits and hacks to manage your time effectively;

- ideas on how you can coach yourself to 'outstanding';

- memory techniques for students;

- literacy in lessons;

- marking and homework.

Ideal for newly qualified teachers, as well as more experienced teachers who are looking for some fresh ideas for their lessons, this highly practical resource will instil the habits that will enable you to perform at an outstanding level consistently in the classroom.

**Mark Harris** is a practising secondary school teacher; he is a Specialist Leader in Education in the Birmingham region. He designs and delivers professional development for schools in this area and is also a guest lecturer in the School of Education at the University of Birmingham, UK.

# How to Develop the Habits of Outstanding Teaching

A practical guide for secondary teachers

**Mark Harris**

Routledge
Taylor & Francis Group

LONDON AND NEW YORK

First published 2016
by Routledge
2 Park Square, Milton Park, Abingdon, Oxon OX14 4RN

and by Routledge
711 Third Avenue, New York, NY 10017

*Routledge is an imprint of the Taylor & Francis Group, an informa business*

*British Library Cataloguing in Publication Data*
A catalogue record for this book is available from the British Library

*Library of Congress Cataloging-in-Publication Data*
Names: Harris, Mark, 1976– author.
Title: How to develop the habits of outstanding teaching : a practical guide for
    secondary teachers / Mark Harris.
Description: Abingdon, Oxon ; New York, NY : Routledge, 2016.
Identifiers: LCCN 2015041197 | ISBN 9781138950467 (hardback) |
    ISBN 9781138950474 (pbk.) | ISBN 9781315668710 (ebook)
Subjects: LCSH: High school teaching. | Effective teaching.
Classification: LCC LB1737 .H37 2016 | DDC 373.1102—dc23
LC record available at http://lccn.loc.gov/2015041197

ISBN: 978-1-138-95046-7 (hbk)
ISBN: 978-1-138-95047-4 (pbk)
ISBN: 978-1-315-66871-0 (ebk)

Typeset in Celeste and Optima
by Apex CoVantage, LLC

MIX
Paper from
responsible sources
FSC® C013056
www.fsc.org

Printed and bound in Great Britain by
TJ International Ltd, Padstow, Cornwall

# Contents

# Contents

# Illustrations

## Figures

## Tables

# Dedication and acknowledgements

## Dedicated to my family

This book contains new teaching strategies along with remodelled and refreshed teaching techniques. Where possible I have acknowledged the source of the idea; however, with the wealth of resources now available to teachers, it is not always feasible to find the original source. Teaching resources results from creativity, synergy from discussions with both staff and student, research and sharing best practice. Therefore, if this book contains an idea not previously acknowledged, I apologise.

I would like to thank the staff I have worked with over the years who have supported me to improve my teaching practice. I would especially like to thank Jean Johnston.

# Introduction

The aim of this book is to help you to become outstanding by providing you with not only outstanding practical teaching strategies but also a number of support mechanisms for both you and your students to help you both excel.

I was once told 'you should aim to take away three good ideas from any book or teaching course you attend'. I hope that this book will provide you with far more than three ideas. To get the most out of this resource, consider the following:

- Keep an open mind.

- Think about how you can relate the ideas to your subject.

- Practise.

As with many things, the success of these habits and strategies will depend on you. It is through practice that these strategies can develop into habits, and once you have instilled outstanding habits, you are more than halfway there. This point cannot be emphasised enough: You must keep practising and never stop learning. Outstanding is a mindset; if you have decided and are prepared to be outstanding, then you know that it is not inborn, but it is the result of endeavour. Practice is key.

## 'Outstanding' is a mindset

The term 'outstanding' has come to mean a lot of things within education and, in reality, has been used by government to represent a fixed set of criteria. Whilst I appreciate why they use the term, their usage should not deter us from exploring the true meaning of the word. We could equally substitute 'outstanding' for 'excellent' or 'exceptional'. Outstanding teaching is outstanding teaching regardless of which educational system or country you teach in. Therefore, this book is not pitched to tick boxes or to meet specific criteria or standards. It is a collection of habits, ideas and strategies that I have developed and continue to use within the classroom today.

You are in an incredibly powerful position. The interactions we have with our students can help to shape their lives; therefore, we should not be flippant with our role. Enthuse, inspire, motivate, create and challenge your students – and they will never forget the positive influence you had on them.

# 1

# How to develop the habits of outstanding teaching

Outstanding teaching is attainable for all teachers. It is not reserved for the lofty few but open for all to achieve. For some it may only require tweaking and developing a few new habits, and for others it may require dedication and a change in mindset to bring about improvements. Whatever the situation you find yourself in, outstanding teaching is not beyond your grasp.

Let us start by considering where you are now in your teaching career and what it is you want to achieve. You may be in one of the following situations:

• New to teaching and keen to develop your teaching practice.

• Teaching for several years and struggling to move your teaching on to the next level.

• Experienced and looking to develop your teaching repertoire further or discover new ideas that enhance your practice.

• Returning to teaching and wanting to update or reinvigorate your teaching practice.

Whatever your personal situation, consider your starting point: Where are you now and what do you want to go on to achieve? To help you review your current position, consider the following question: If you overheard students talking about you in the playground or on the street, what would they be saying about you? Reflect on this for a while. It is a question to get you thinking about how you are perceived as a teacher. Are you the strict teacher, the fun teacher, the clever teacher or the grumpy teacher? Having thought about this question, now consider: How do you want to be remembered by the students in the future? The reality is that you never forget an outstanding teacher. In some cases, it is those outstanding teachers who have inspired us to enter the profession. So, do you want to be an outstanding teacher who inspires or be remembered as Mr/Mrs Grumpy? It's never too late to change and become the kind of teacher that you dream you can be.

## How to coach yourself to outstanding

The good news is that you already possess everything you need to be outstanding: It is all within you. What you have to do is develop your mindset to allow yourself to achieve your ambitions. This idea can be both liberating and scary, but 'outstanding' is a state of mind. You may not be outstanding yet because you haven't decided to be. Once you make the decision to be 'outstanding', commit to it. Go to the edge of your comfort zone and see what you can achieve. It cannot be any worse than where you are now, can it?

Teaching can be a strange profession. After one year of training on the job, you are considered expert enough to be left to your own devices and pretty much told to 'get on with it'. Only when something goes wrong does it necessitate some form of training or support. If you are lucky enough for nothing to go wrong, then you can go merrily on your way, only attending the compulsory training day at the start of the year when the hot topic of conversation is where everybody went on holiday and what you think of the new cakes.

I'm thankful to say that in recent years the culture of training has shifted rapidly. It needs to. This does not mean that training should concentrate on every new pedagogical idea that comes along; rather, it should focus on individualised training programmes to help all teachers to improve their performance in the classroom in order to enable their students to make progress. Regardless of the training/coaching programme that operates at your school, the best approach is for you to take ownership of your own development. Become your own coach and train yourself to peak performance.

Ask yourself the following questions:

- What do outstanding teachers do?
- What do they do differently to you?
- What's holding you back?

## What does outstanding look like?

I believe that outstanding teachers have two key aspects that make them excel: character traits and teaching habits/skills. In many ways, the two are intertwined: for example, outstanding teachers characteristically have strong will power that results in resilience and the ability to build new habits and learn new skills. However, if we dissect these features and strip out complexity, I believe that outstanding teachers can be created. Start by considering the following two questions:

- What are the characteristics of outstanding teachers?
- What do outstanding teachers do that make them outstanding?

Although this list is by no means comprehensive, I assume that the following traits appear on many lists:

**Traits of outstanding teachers**

- Well organised

- Enthusiastic

- Knowledgeable

- Inspiring

- Positive

- Honest

- Good rapport

In addition to these traits, there are a number of habits that outstanding teachers possess. It is important to recognise that outstanding teachers, whilst being proficient in many of these habits/skills, will not necessarily be outstanding in all areas. In fact, they may only excel in a handful of skills, yet be considered outstanding because they optimise their 'best' skills and work to develop those skills they consider less defined. To become outstanding, it is important not to neglect those skills you already possess. In fact, it is vital that you develop and practise those skills to enhance them even more because this is how you become outstanding – not only by learning new skills but also by refining those skills that you consider to already be your greatest assets.

## How am I doing?

To help you to identify areas of development as well as those skills you are proficient at, rate yourself against the following micro skills. You may need to familiarise yourself with some skills by referring to the appropriate section/chapter in the book first before you complete the survey. In addition to your self-review, ask other trusted colleagues to rate your skills. I appreciate this can be uncomfortable, but it is important to know that your judgements are correct and know how your teaching is perceived. It may be the case that there are glaring discrepancies between what you think of your teaching and the views of others. You need to reflect on this. Your first response may be that 'they don't know what they are talking about'; move beyond this and think carefully about how you deliver that skill. It may become clear that you are going about it in the wrong way. If you really want substantial data to analyse, ask a number of colleagues to complete the form anonymously or even ask students as well.

The list of micro skills aims to break down and deconstruct fundamental components of outstanding teaching. Rather than saying 'I need to improve my questioning', which is a large teaching and learning area, it is more beneficial to say 'I need to improve on engaging all students when questioning'. This is a far more achievable goal and highlights a specific area of development. Once you have mastered this component of questioning, then you can move on work on to another element of teaching practice.

The micro skills sheet should also highlight areas of strength. Exploit these skills: Utilise your existing skills, which have proven to be successful, and get even better at them. Practise and hone these skills further; make yourself an expert of a particular element of teaching practice. Become world class in one particular area and I am confident it will improve your overall teaching practice. Plus, you become the 'go-to person' for marking, for example, or the 'master' of questioning.

**Table 1.1** Micro skills

| Micro skills: How good are you at the following?: | Score: 10 being the highest | | | | | | | | | |
|---|---|---|---|---|---|---|---|---|---|---|
| | 1 | 2 | 3 | 4 | 5 | 6 | 7 | 8 | 9 | 10 |
| Planning: Writing outcome-oriented lesson objectives. | | | | | | | | | | |
| Planning: Writing engaging learning questions. | | | | | | | | | | |
| Planning: Writing success criteria to challenge all students. | | | | | | | | | | |
| Planning: Planning takes account of misconceptions and gaps in learning informed by previous learning. | | | | | | | | | | |
| Starters: Challenges are designed to 'hook' students and they link up students' learning and create curiosity. | | | | | | | | | | |
| Starters: You allow time for students to 'reflect and correct' their work. | | | | | | | | | | |
| Success criteria: Your success criteria are designed to challenge all students. | | | | | | | | | | |
| Success criteria: You refer to criteria within the lesson and students are confident at using them to improve their own performance. | | | | | | | | | | |
| Differentiation: You offer a range of devices to support low ability students. | | | | | | | | | | |
| Differentiation: You offer a range of devices to support students with additional needs. | | | | | | | | | | |
| Differentiation: You offer a range of devices to stretch the most able students. | | | | | | | | | | |
| Modelling: You model work to provide support and scaffolding, allowing students to achieve excellence. | | | | | | | | | | |
| Independent learning: You provide opportunity for students to take ownership of their own learning and develop skills to create autonomy. | | | | | | | | | | |
| Questioning: You use devices to include all students when questioning. | | | | | | | | | | |
| Questioning: You ask a range of questions to develop students' thinking, including open and closed questions with a range of levels from Bloom's Taxonomy. | | | | | | | | | | |
| Questioning: You set standards for students' responses, including answering in full sentences and using formal language. | | | | | | | | | | |
| Questioning: You differentiate your questioning to challenge all students. | | | | | | | | | | |
| Questioning: You question to check understanding and highlight any misconceptions or gaps in learning. | | | | | | | | | | |

| | Score: 10 being the highest | | | | | | | | | |
|---|---|---|---|---|---|---|---|---|---|---|
| Literacy (speaking): You use a range of devices to encourage students to participate in speaking activities. | | | | | | | | | | |
| Literacy (speaking): You set standards for oral participation, including the use of key words. | | | | | | | | | | |
| Literacy (reading): You use a range of devices to engage students with reading activities. | | | | | | | | | | |
| Literacy (reading): You use a range of devices to check students' understanding and comprehension of what they have read. | | | | | | | | | | |
| Literacy (writing): You provide opportunities for students to write with extension. | | | | | | | | | | |
| Literacy (writing): You discuss with students how to structure their written work. | | | | | | | | | | |
| Literacy (writing): You differentiate writing challenges and provide support devices for groups of students, including writing frames, sentence stems and literacy mats. | | | | | | | | | | |
| Literacy (writing): You model work to demonstrate standards. | | | | | | | | | | |
| Challenge: You offer a range of challenges and activities within your lessons to engage all students. | | | | | | | | | | |
| Challenge: You manage time well and you have set routines so that transition between challenges and activities are swift. | | | | | | | | | | |
| Challenge: You manage group work activities well. | | | | | | | | | | |
| Assessment and feedback: You use differentiated target questions for students to respond to. | | | | | | | | | | |
| Assessment and feedback: You use success criteria when marking to inform students of where they are and what they need to do to improve their performance. | | | | | | | | | | |
| Assessment and feedback: You provide students with targets to improve their work. | | | | | | | | | | |
| Assessment and feedback: You provide opportunity for students to action their targets. | | | | | | | | | | |
| Assessment and feedback: You provide opportunities for students to self and peer assess. | | | | | | | | | | |
| Assessment and feedback: You model what 'good' self and peer assessment involves and includes. | | | | | | | | | | |
| Plenaries: You use a range of plenary devices to consolidate students' understanding. | | | | | | | | | | |
| Homework: Your homework challenges are differentiated to meet the needs of all students. | | | | | | | | | | |
| Homework: You offer your students a range of homework challenges and activities. | | | | | | | | | | |

## How to be your own teaching coach

### Goals

One of the first things you need to develop is total clarity about what you want to achieve. It is not sufficient to simply say 'I want to be outstanding'; your goals need to be more tangible than that. Be specific in your goals. Write them down in the present tense. These actions will set your mind working on these aims. Try to make your goals measurable so that you can chart your progress and see incremental improvements.

Examples of teaching goals you may set:

- Achieve three 'outstanding' lesson observations this year.

- My students achieve an average 8 point score.

- Achieve 100% A* – C grade.

- All of my students make three levels of progress.

For the sake of this exercise, we will use the following goal:

- Achieve three 'outstanding' lesson observations this year.

Having set your goals and the time frame you are working in, get to work on planning how you will achieve these goals.

## Plan

Having decided on your goal, you need to plan for how you are going to achieve it. 'Outstanding' doesn't just happen; it is the result of small incremental improvements created during practice and instilling successful habits that you first need to identify. To support this process, the coaching sheet in Table 1.2 will help you to document and record your improvements.

**Table 1.2**  The coaching sheet

| Goal: Achieve three outstanding lesson observations this year. | | | | |
|---|---|---|---|---|
| **Target area to work on:** Questioning<br>**Micro skill:** Ask high level questions to develop students' thinking<br>**Feedback/even better if . . . (EBI):**<br>EBI students prioritise their answers rather than giving a general response, so they can develop deeper thinking.<br>**Scheduled incremental improvement** | | | | |
| Lesson 1 | Lesson 2 | Lesson 3 | Lesson 4 | Lesson 5 |
| 9A: Use the following question stems:<br>Prioritise . . .<br>Suggest way to improve . . .<br>What makes that a good answer? | 7T: Use the following question stems:<br>Prioritise . . .<br>Which answer did you like best? | PLANNING LESSON | 11S: Use the following question stems:<br>Prioritise . . .<br>How could we solve . . .?<br>What makes that a good answer? | 8A: Use the following question stems:<br>Prioritise . . .<br>Give me an answer with the word *metaphor* in it. |
| **Feedback: What went well (WWW):** | | | | |
| **Feedback: Even better if . . . (EBI):** | | | | |

**Goal:** The overall goal you are going to achieve written in the present tense.

**Target area to work on:** The larger teaching component that you have highlighted to address.

**Micro skill:** This is the smaller element of the teaching skill recognised as needing improvement.

**Feedback/even better if (EBI):** Having either self-assessed or received peer assessment of your teaching practice, you may have identified areas that still require improving or tweaking. Writing these points in this section gives you something to work on.

**Scheduled incremental improvement:** Concentrate on just one or two aspects of the micro skill. There are a number of ways you could use questioning to develop students' thinking, but just focusing on using a select few question stems allows you to develop the habit of using them consistently in your teaching. As you will notice, to address the 'even better if' statement I have used the question stem 'prioritise' consistently throughout, to really target and improve this one area of teaching practice that needs improving. Using this stem in every teaching lesson will help to develop the habit to automaticity.

**What went well (WWW):** It is important to celebrate success. If the questioning aspect of your teaching went well that day, record it. Which part of your questioning went well? Why do you think this was the case? What did you do that made it so successful? This reflection gives you the thinking and processing time to identify and recognise what facet of your teaching went well so that you may replicate it in future lessons.

Great coaches ask great questions, so when you have finished your day or while you are driving home, reflect on the following questions. Your answers will then help you to take steps forward and make those small incremental gains towards mastery.

**Coaching questions:**

- How would you rate your teaching today?
- What did you learn?
- If it were an ideal day, what would that look like?
- What can you do tomorrow to make that a reality?
- What is the next step you need to make to improve?

## How to develop outstanding habits

Outstanding teaching is the result of developing outstanding habits. A habit can be defined as: *an acquired pattern of behaviour that has become almost involuntary as a result of frequent repetition.* (www.thefreedictionary.com).

Outstanding teachers have the knack of making it look easy to observers. The reality, of course, is that they have worked very hard to develop the habits and skills that allow them to operate certain procedures with automaticity whilst their mind is engaged on another task. For example, an outstanding teacher may have developed the habit of asking a range of high level questions automatically when questioning students. This allows the teacher to listen carefully to the student response so they can develop the learning further, rather than having to concentrate on asking gradually harder questions and thus not listening intently to the students' responses (which would lead them to miss key opportunities to develop learning further). It is the ability to develop automaticity in certain aspects of the lesson that will free your mind to concentrate on other aspects of it. Habits and automaticity can only be developed with practice and conscious thought. You must consciously think about how you react to certain cues so that with time they become an automatic feature of your teaching practice. Your current teaching practice is essentially the sum of your current habits. How you consistently react to situations and stimuli governs your comfort zone. Be opened minded to the following ideas, push your boundaries and stick with it until you have developed habits that make you outstanding.

Charles Duhigg (*The Power of Habit*, 2013) recognised that habit has three specific features: cues, routine and reward.

**Cues:** These are triggers that stimulate a response from you.

**Routine:** How we respond to the cue.

**Reward:** The reward you give yourself that helps your brain to remember that habit for the future.

The example below is a typical scenario in the classroom:

- The cue is a student who starts to talk when the teacher is giving out instructions.

- The routine is that the teacher stops talking, reminds the student that talking is not appropriate and that it is not part of the class rules, and that it is important to listen so that he/she understands what to do in the next challenge.

- The reward is that the teacher has regained control of the class and all students are able to hear the instructions so that they can complete the challenge successfully.

It is important to note that poor habits will still provide a reward. If we consider the same cue: The student talks over the teacher but, in this instance, the teacher's routine is to ignore the poor behaviour and simply talk louder. The reward for the teacher is avoiding potential conflict with a student. Obviously, this is not the preferred way to achieve an outcome, but the teacher still receives a perceived reward, and it is this perceived reward that creates entrenched habits and behaviours.

So the key to developing new habits or fixing bad habits is to consider our routine/response to cues. There are several cues that will stimulate a routine. These are:

- Location: How you react to a certain place. Consider your own school: Are there certain locations around school where students are poorly behaved or areas/classrooms where they appear to be calmer?

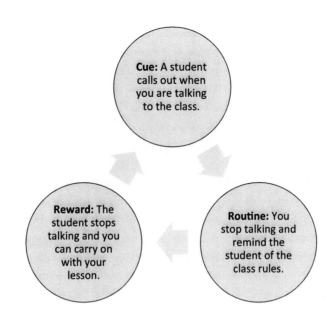

**Figure 1.1**   The habit loop

- Time: Do you react differently to the same scenario at different times of the day?

- Emotion.

- Other people's action: How do we react to students' behaviour?

- Our own (immediately preceding) action.

## Develop habits so you are able to operate with automaticity

Start by identifying a new habit you want to instil. What is it in your current practice that needs improving? Below are a number of common habits that teachers feel they need to establish or improve. Write your own in the present tense.

- All students listen carefully when I speak.

- I ask a range of questions to challenge all students.

- I involve all students when questioning.

- I differentiate my lessons so the students are appropriately challenged.

- My marking informs the students of what they need to do to improve their work.

- I give time within lessons for students to action their feedback.

**Why bother?** The first thing you need to consider is this: What is the point of developing this new habit? It has to be important to you; don't just try to change your practice because somebody tells you that you should. You have to 'buy in' to the new habit; think about the reward you will receive if you can ingrain the habit or how good you will feel if you know you have stopped a bad habit. Remind yourself constantly about why you are doing this and keep the end goal in mind.

**Start small:** Complexity is the enemy of execution. If it is too convoluted or elaborate, the chances of you bothering to attempt the new habit will diminish. Make it really simple and small; once this is automatic, then you can develop the habit further.

**Reminders:** Set up a system of reminders to support you in the developmental stage. These may be sticky notes or visual reminders to stimulate you to use your new habit. For example: When I was trying to develop my questioning technique, I stuck a brightly coloured card to my desk with three question stems I wanted to use in each lesson. Then whenever I was by my desk I was reminded to use those questions. Starting with just three questions made it simple and manageable, and therefore it never felt too onerous to engage with the new habit. Over time those three questions became automatic, allowing me to add two more questions to my repertoire, and the process was repeated.

**Create links:** Link your new habit to habits you already have in place. For instance, if you want to develop students' recall and consolidate their learning from previous lessons, one device you can use is a short, five-question quiz. Link this short quiz habit to a habit you already have, such as taking the class register. So every time you finish your register you instantly move on to a quick quiz to test students' recall.

The old habits that you link new ones to need to be ones you are confident you do on a regular basis – ideally daily. This may be applied at home as well. So whenever you brush your teeth, you quickly think about the lessons you have that day and confirm in your mind that you have all the resources you need for those lessons. When driving home, every time you reach a particular junction or set of traffic lights, you stop to consider one thing that went well that day.

**Secret reminders:** These are particularly effective when dealing with behavioural issues. Have your own personal secret gesture or location that calms you down when you are feeling stressed. I had a colleague who would rub his ear lobe whenever he was feeling annoyed and this simple gesture alone would calm him down. Have a spot on the carpet where you stand and take deep breaths to regain control or refocus yourself. Alternatively, use the spot on the carpet to ask higher level questioning or to remind yourself to discuss the success criteria used in the lesson. Whatever you use your secret reminders for, make them simple and make them work for you.

Some of the above techniques may work for you and some may not. You may need to experiment until you find a cue that works. Developing a habit is a process, and depending on which scientific journal you read, it can take anywhere from 21 to 66 days to properly develop new habits and create new neurological grooves in your brain. It's not easy, but consider the intrinsic rewards, and if you stutter and forget the procedures for a few days, don't beat yourself up and stop. Reflect on what you need to do to improve next time and get going again. Developing excellent habits is the only thing stopping you from becoming outstanding, so keep going! You can do it!

**How to develop the habits of outstanding teaching in a nutshell**

- Outstanding teaching is a mindset.

- Become your own teaching coach: Identify areas to work on and get practicing.

- Practice makes progress: Get feedback on how you are doing and then tweak your practice to improve.

- Set yourself a goal and achieve daily incremental improvements; you will soon get there.

- Develop habits that allow you to operate with automaticity.

- Develop better habits by changing you routines to cues.

- Stick with it!

**Figure 1.2**  How to develop the habits of outstanding teaching, in a nutshell

# 2

# Lesson planning

Lesson planning is fundamental to consistent outstanding teaching. If you are new to the profession, then lesson planning may appear laborious and time consuming, but as with everything in this book the more you practise the better you become. In time, you may not need to include all the features of the lesson in your plan because some have become automatic habits of your teaching practice. The purpose of the plan is to provide direction for your teaching so that everything you do is focused on student progress.

When I first started teaching, my planning was mostly centred on me: What would I say to the students? How would I start the lesson? What exciting activities would I deliver? It wasn't until later that I begin to change my mindset from 'I' to 'them'. What starter activity would help 'hook' them in? What activities will help them understand? What questions will push them on? Once I began planning with the students' understanding and progress in mind, I found that the whole process falls into place, creating a better flow in a lesson that has far more impact on student achievement and performance.

Lesson planning is like setting goals for the students without them knowing yet. As with any type of goal setting, you begin with the end in mind: What results are you trying to achieve? If you are clear about the lesson goal or outcome, then everything else can be built around this. As mentioned earlier, this may be a mind shift for you. I myself would rarely consider what I wanted the students to achieve; I was caught up thinking about what I was going to achieve. My internal monologue would be, 'I'm teaching volcanoes tomorrow. I'll put on a video clip to begin with, then I'll get them to answer questions 1–5 from the textbook, and I'll finish off with a poster on volcanoes' and as long as they all completed the work and behaved themselves, I judged that a very successful lesson. Yet although the students may have completed all the work and sat there quietly, did they really understand any of it? Was it challenging enough for all students? How would they remember anything they learned during the lesson?

## Stage 1: Objective

The first thing to consider is this: What do you want your students to know or be able to do by the end of the lesson? This should be linked to the syllabus/specification and tied to the longer term goal which is likely to be that all your students achieve their aspirational target grades/scores. There is little point making this objective too grand or all encompassing; the aim is to produce small incremental gains, allowing the students to master a certain aspect of the course before moving on. It is also worth remembering at this point that progress is not linear. Students will not progress at a uniform or proportional amount each lesson. In fact, in some lessons they may appear to be making little progress whilst in other lessons students may be making huge bounds in their knowledge and understanding. Think back to when you learned to drive. If you are anything like me, in some lessons I struggled to make any progress and I was left thinking, 'I will never do this.' Then, in another lesson, everything clicked and I was making rapid progress.

Having considered what you want the students to know or be able to do by the end of the lesson, you also need to consider the following questions in tandem: What's the point? Why do they need to learn this? How does this relate to the big picture of what you teach? Are you able to justify to yourself and the students exactly why they are learning what you are about to teach them?

Whatever objective you set, make sure it is measurable. Students need to be able to demonstrate whether or not they have mastered the skills or demonstrate that they have understood the content. As the teacher, you need to know how students are progressing, which students have mastered the concepts, ideas or skills and also which students require support and time to fully do so. This will then inform your planning for the next lesson. Are there aspects of the lesson you need to go over again? How will you consolidate the learning that has occurred? Will students be given the opportunity to apply what they have learn? All these questions will need to be considered.

**Useful objective stems:**

You may find it useful to use stems such as 'By the end of the lesson you will . . .'

- **know that . . .** (knowledge and content-based information)

- **understand how/why . . .** (understanding and comprehension of concepts, ideas and processes)

- **develop / be able to . . .** (skill acquisition and understanding)

- **develop / be aware of . . .** (values and attitudes, empathy, global citizenship, others' views, conflict of opinion)

An alternative is to phrase objectives in terms of the stem 'We are learning to . . . so that . . .'

# Stage 2: Learning question

Having defined your lesson objective, the learning question you pose aims to create curiosity and engage your students to the lesson. Turning your objective into a learning question helps to 'hook' students as well as make it more accessible and interesting. Having surveyed students, I find they say that lesson objectives are often bland and boring whilst the question stimulates intrigue and interest.

## Examples

The objective of the lesson is for the students to know and understand the effects of a volcanic eruption. A fitting title might be 'Effects of volcanoes'. However, think how the students will react to the following learning questions: What are the effects of volcanic eruption? Or, to make it even more interesting: How did Harry Truman die? This last question allows you to develop your teaching to include case study material from the 1980 eruption of Mount St. Helens, which killed 56 people, whilst also building in the content surrounding the effects of volcanic eruptions.

As well as making your lesson more interesting to the students, the question's other major benefit is that it acts as a bookend to the lesson. You begin the lesson with the learning question and then end the lesson by returning to the same question. Referring to the learning question during the plenary allows you to evidence clear progress or inform you of misconceptions or gaps in student learning. A plenary activity may be to write a paragraph answering the learning question. This shows the progress of your students and allows you to read their work to check their understanding, thus informing your next lesson. Did they all get it? If not, why not? What do I need to do next lesson to make sure they understand it?

## Stage 3: Starter

You must begin by considering how you will introduce the lesson. How can you 'hook' them in? This may be an engaging starter activity or it may be an opportunity for students to reflect and improve upon their previous work. Whichever device you use, it should put the lesson into context for the students and relate to the bigger picture of what you are trying to achieve.

Great starter activities challenge student thinking, provoke curiosity and link to students' previous or future learning. They should be pacey and snappy and set the tone for the lesson to come. Starter ideas and support can be found in Chapter 3.

## Stage 4: Success Criteria

This is such an important feature of outstanding lessons that I have dedicated a chapter to it. The key idea is that both you and the students need to know what success looks like and what they need to do to achieve it. The second aim of well-designed success criteria is to inspire and support students to achieve higher standards – not to accept mediocrity and instead strive for excellence.

## Stage 5: Challenges

The challenges or activities for the student to complete will often form the main body of the lesson. They should be designed to complement and support what you are hoping to achieve. The challenges should fit the learning objective rather than the learning objective fitting around the activities. Remember, it is all about student progress, so how will your challenges help to develop students' understanding or skill mastery? Linked to these challenges will be your use of success criteria, differentiation and evidence of progress.

Below are a number of questions to help you develop challenges aimed at improving students' performance and enhancing their progress.

- How will your activity help to achieve the learning objective?

- How will it operate? If the activity involves group work, will this be based on ability or friendship groups? What are the logistics of the activity? How will you give out the equipment?

- How will you differentiate the challenge so it is appropriate for all students?

- How will you support low ability students and how will you stretch the higher ability?

- What high order questions will you ask?

- What do you predict the answers to be? How will you resolve any misconceptions?

- How will the students demonstrate what they have learned?

- How will you check their progress?

- Is there an opportunity to develop their literacy or numeracy skills?

- Is there an opportunity for students to consolidate or apply their learning?

- How will students know if they have been successful?

- What are the barriers to learning? What will stop this lesson from being successful?

- What can I do to remove those barriers?

Please note I would not expect you to write an answer to each of these questions; they are simply meant to stimulate thought and positive action. I also would not necessarily expect your lesson to contain all of the above points. It is not realistic to expect every lesson to be fully differentiated, with opportunities to develop literacy and numeracy while both consolidating and applying all the content within a lesson. However, if you have considered all of the above questions, then you will have planned the lesson well. The questions are there to ensure you do not miss a trick and that no opportunity to improve the students' performance is missed.

Empathise with the students when considering challenges. Are the activities you are planning interesting and enjoyable? Not every lesson can be, but avoid delivering the same type of lesson time and time again. Variety is the spice of life, and you may find that a new approach is all that is needed to reignite or create a spark in your students. Chunk activities, if you find this works well, to keep your students engaged and on task with the learning. Breaking up a large concept or idea makes it far more accessible for the students, and they will generally participate more.

# Stage 6: Questioning

Planning high order questions is an outstanding habit to cultivate. High order questions guarantee high order thinking and responses, skills we are keen to develop with our students. Mapping out what questions you will be asking (and when) steers the lesson toward excellence, creating increasing levels of challenge for all students, and supports improvements in performance. Two or three high order questions may be all that is necessary to create further curiosity or to challenge the students to think at a higher level. The chapter on questioning will help you to develop and implement this vital skill of outstanding teaching.

# Stage 7: Plenary

This is the stage where students may have the opportunity to demonstrate what they have learned or to consolidate or apply their knowledge, understanding or skill. Do not underestimate the impact of a well-designed plenary. It supports recall, helps to consolidate the learning that has taken place and can help to commit learning to long term memory. It is important to set adequate time aside to complete this stage. In the past, it was often advised that plenaries should be approximately 5 minutes long. I have no fixed time limit on plenaries; sometimes you may only need 2 or 3 minutes to cover what the students learned in the lesson. However, in the majority of cases, to have any real impact plenaries may require up to 10 minutes. Obviously, it depends on the lesson and what the students have been learning, but they should not be prescriptive or simply an add-on to the lesson. The plenaries chapter contains a number of ideas to guide your students toward peak performance and to aid their progress.

Class_____     Subject_____     Lesson_____

Learning Question: *What do I want them to learn?*

Objectives: *What do I want them to know or be able to do by the end of the lesson? (content/ skills) The advantage of this question is that it is measurable.*

What's the point? (To be able to . . .) (So that . . .) *How does this relate to them, how does it relate to the last lesson, the big picture?*

**Success Criteria**

- How will **they** know they have been successful?
- How will **you** know they have been successful?
- What does success look like?

| Success criteria: | Level/Grade/Score |
|---|---|
| | |
| | |
| | |

**Starter**

- How will I introduce the lesson?
- How can I 'hook' them in?
- Make sure it's short and snappy.

Ideas: Picture, text, experiment, demo, exam question/challenge question, quote, model, 'what do you think of when . . .?'

**Challenges/Activities**

- What do I want them to be learning about?
- How does this link to my objective/learning question?

- How can I differentiate the task to make it 'appropriately challenging' for all groups of students (most able, least able, additional needs)?

- How will this look? (Group work – grouped on ability or mixed? – individual work, card sort, experiment, practical, exam question, creative lesson)

Ideas:

- How can I make sure they all understand what they need to do?

- How do I want this work to look in their books? (Presentation of work)

- How can I support the least able or students with additional needs? (Students to repeat instructions on the task, lead learners, work in pairs)

- Is it challenging for all students? Are *all* students stretched? What if some students finish the work?

- How will I check their progress?

- What 'stretching' questions can I ask?

Questions: (examples)
Can you predict . . .
What solutions would you suggest . . .
What facts show that . . .
What would happen if . . .

Is there an opportunity to develop literacy or mathematics?

- List of key words

- Model work

- Students answer in sentences

- Skimming, scanning

- Formal language

- How will the students know if they have been successful? (Students reflect on their learning WWW, EBI, peer/self-assessment)

- What are the barriers to this being a successful lesson? (Poor behaviour, students off task, students do not understand the activity)

- How can I remove those barriers?

**Assessment and feedback**

- Targets to achieve
- Previous targets have been actioned
- Marking for SPAG

**Homework**

- Does the homework support the learning in the classroom?
- Is it challenging for all groups of students (most and least able, students with additional needs)?

**Teaching assistants and students with additional needs**

- How will I use the TA within my lesson to make the most impact upon learning?
- How will they use the classroom support plan?
- Is my lesson dyslexia friendly? (Individual sheets, comic sans font, visual prompts)
- Is my text accessible? (Readability)

**Figure 2.1**   Lesson planning support sheet

**Planning, in a nutshell**

- Proper preparation prevents a poor performance.
- Have total clarity on what you want to achieve by the end of the lesson.
- Use learning questions to create curiosity and to engage the students.
- Design success criteria so both you and the students know what success looks like.
- Create challenges that are accessible and challenging for all. It doesn't matter if they do not get the skills, ideas or concepts first time. Progress often involves failure, struggle and resilience.
- Plan your questions and predict the responses.
- Consider the barriers to the lesson being a success and then put in plans to mitigate against those barriers.
- Use plenaries to 'book end' the lesson.
- If you have a teaching assistant, plan to utilise him or her and get the assistant involved throughout the lesson.

**Figure 2.2**   Planning, in a nutshell

# 3

# Starters

There is a plethora of starter teaching resources on the internet, in books and shared in staffrooms, that makes this an area many teachers feel they deliver well. However, this can become an overlooked and often unplanned part of the lesson, with many preferring to concentrate on the main body of the lesson rather than the beginning. The importance of an excellent starter cannot be overlooked. So whether you are new to teaching or a teacher who feels competent with starter activities, I hope the following section will allow you to reconsider the importance of a starter or reinvigorate your starter activities.

For me, the starter has several important purposes:

- To engage and 'hook' the students by creating curiosity.

- To provide an opportunity for students to action feedback.

- To contextualise the lesson.

- To set the pace and tone of the lesson.

The aim is to have the starter activity either on the board or in front of the students as soon as they enter the room. It should require minimal instruction so that they can just get on with the challenge. It is important that the starter requires very little input from the teacher. Ideally the majority of the class should be engaged in the activity whilst the teacher deals with any housekeeping issues, such handing out paper to the student who has forgotten the book, lending pens or dealing with uniform issues.

## Logistics of starters

There are three key features of classroom practice that will ensure that your lesson starts with purpose:

1. Have the activity on the board prior to the students entering the classroom so that there is something for them to do as soon as they enter the room. Make sure that there are clear instructions and that the activity is accessible to all students.

2. Have the students' books on their tables ready for them. Put them out before the first lesson, at break and lunchtimes and at the very end of the previous lesson whilst the class is packing away. This helps to support classroom behaviour, since students are not wandering around the classroom and neither are they idly chatting whilst waiting for their books to begin their work. It establishes purpose and ensures your lesson begins efficiently.

3. Have paper on your desk and pens available, ready to distribute as necessary.

If these three things are in place, it allows you to greet students at the door whilst the others are immediately engaged in a learning activity. The key is to make this routine. If students know that once they enter the classroom there is an expectation that they should immediately engage and get on with a challenge, it settles students quickly and you are able to swiftly proceed with the lesson.

## Engage and hook: nine super quick and simple devices

Engaging and hooking students can be achieved in a vast variety of ways, from using a simple picture to promote discussion, to the teacher eating a mashed up Mars bar from a cleaned-out dog food can to create the 'ewww' factor. (This technique was used by a colleague who then proceeded to discuss misconceptions.) Whatever device you decide upon, it should be delivered with pace and enthusiasm. I have a presentation with the following nine devices already on as a template; therefore, when I need to I can simply change the component of the starter, and I have a brand new challenge. The benefits are twofold: The teacher saves preparation time and the students have an understanding of how the activity works – consequently, they require little instruction and they are able to begin straight away.

### 1) 'Picture this'

The advantage of a picture is that it can promote a great deal of discussion. Use it to stimulate interest and develop understanding of your chosen topic by asking a series of questions to get your students thinking. Look at the examples below and the questions used by the teacher to promote discussion and deeper thinking.

What would you:

- See?
- Hear?
- Smell?
- Feel?

**Figure 3.1**   Picture this

What surprises you about the picture?

What links you to the picture?

Additional 'challenge' questions may follow. A favourite of mine is, 'What do you think is happening outside of the photograph?' This engages the students and challenges them to contextualise the photo. They have to think what else might be going on or consider the location of the picture. For this example, other follow-up questions may include:

'What's happening further up the road? Where does the road lead to'?

This can be followed up by more challenging questions:

'Prioritise the problems of traffic congestion'? 'How could you improve the lives of the inhabitants?'

2)   **Would you rather . . .?**

This is a simple starter that has huge impact. From the teacher's point of view, it is an easy set up. You simply think of two conflicting ideas or concepts and ask the students to respond to the question, 'Would you rather . . .?' Their response can be either verbal or written; you may want them to discuss it in pairs or work individually. There are many options. Set clear expectations – for example, 'I want you to write a minimum of six lines in your book' or 'You must answer in full sentences'. I'm confident that their responses will be inspiring and unexpected.

Some examples from different subject areas include asking: Would you rather . . .

- be a Capulet or a Montague? (English)
- fight for Lancashire or Yorkshire during the war of the Roses? (History)
- be an endomorph or an ectomorph body type? (PE)
- live in the Amazon rainforest or the Himalayas? (Geography)
- all people belong to a religion or there were no religions? (RE)

3) **What if . . .?**

This idea is adapted from a Mike Gershon starter activity. (www.mikegershon.com) Students are required to consider the outcomes and consequences of a particular event or scenario. This may be a statement, linked to a picture, or a short video. It promotes deeper thinking and requires students to consciously evaluate a situation or circumstance. Students may be asked to respond verbally or in their books, work as a pair, in groups or individually. Again the aim is for the quick starter to engage and hook the students. I find that this activity meets both criteria wonderfully.

Some examples from different subject areas: What if . . .

- we had another ice age? (Geography)
- we could eradicate malaria? (Science)
- there were no religions? (RE)
- Harold had won the Battle of Hastings? (History)
- all the carnivores were absent from a food chain? (Science)
- athletes could use performance enhancing drugs? (PE)

WARNING: In my experience, these starter activity examples can be inspiring, compelling and contagious. The enthusiasm and discussions can spread quickly and you can find that you have spent twenty minutes on just one question. Not that there is anything wrong with this, in my opinion: Why would you want to quash students' passion and enthusiasm for a topic? I say it only to make you aware so that the activity does not railroad you from what you believe to be the crux of the lesson.

4) **What happens next . . .?**

For this activity, students are challenged to predict what happens next. This could be linked to a piece of text that you ask the students to read through first, and then you pose the question. You may use a range of media to set up the activity, including video clips, screen shots from a text message or a Twitter feed. For each medium, students have to predict the next stage or consider what happens next.

A flow chart describing a process or a series of calculations are also useful stems to develop this starter challenge further.

5) **Grandma went to market**

You probably played this memory game as a child, and it certainly has a place in the modern classroom, testing recall and building memory. It is based on the game that begins, 'grandma went to market'; you then add an item (for example, she bought eggs) and then the next student must repeat the item and add another item to the list. You then work your way around the class with each student contributing to the list. This can be adapted to any subject, so instead of 'grandma went to market' it can become:

- I went on a geography field trip to a river valley and I saw . . .

- I cooked a curry and my ingredients were . . .

- I am Macbeth and I . . .

- In my orchestra I have the following instruments . . .

6) **Back-to-back descriptions**

This is a fun way to challenge your students whilst also improving their communication skills. Ask students to sit back to back, and then ask one student to describe what he/she can see in a picture. This picture can be pre-chosen or simply from a page in a textbook. To enhance and add challenge to this activity, students can be asked to used subject-specific terms or, alternately, they can be banned from using certain words in their description. This can then be followed up with questions about the success of the activity. What went well? What were the best descriptions? What made them so good? Which words did they use? To reduce your preparation time, ask students to collect pictures on a particular theme for you as homework. These can then be used in the next lesson by collecting them, mixing them up and then redistributing or using them for another lesson.

7) **Just a minute**

For this challenge students are given one minute to talk to their partner about a chosen topic. This could be what they learned last lesson, what they already know about a particular subject or a what they see in a picture displayed on the board. As students develop their communication skills, I introduce more conditions to the task. They have to talk for a minute without hesitation or repetition. Then they have to use a selection of key words in their monologue. The challenges can become harder as they begin to master the skills. To involve the students who are passively listening, I ask them to tally up the number of key words their partner has used. Then they swap over. For me, that is two minutes of quality learning involving recall of information, knowledge of a particular topic, sufficient understanding to be able to explain to another student – as well as the various literacy skills of talking in sentences, using specialist terms and connectives.

8) **May the force be with you!**

Just as Luke Skywalker used the 'force' in *Star Wars* to predict his opponents' moves, so do the students have to use their powers of telepathy and heightened senses for this activity. This challenge involves students having to recreate a picture, image, diagram or sketch without being able to see what they are drawing. The students poke a pencil half way through a piece of paper to create a shield so they are unable to see what they are drawing underneath. Then ask the students to draw a picture or diagram they created in a previous lesson. They are challenged to try to recall the features of the diagram for their copy or memorise the image they have just seen. Alternative approaches include having the picture, image, diagram or sketch already on the board for them to copy. Or you may ask a partner to describe the image from their book whilst the student attempts to draw it. Or ask the students to study a number of objects to draw before concealing them. This activity works well because it tests the student's power of recall, and they have to carefully consider each pencil mark – more so than if we simply ask them to draw a picture off the board.

9) **Reflect and Correct**: An opportunity for students to action feedback

Not every lesson can start with a fun and entertaining starter activity. Sometimes students need the time to reflect and correct their work. The beginning of the lesson is a golden opportunity for this to take place. I call it 'Reflect and Correct'. This is a chance for student to correct any errors in their work, including spelling, punctuation and grammatical errors; answer any target questions you may have set; and reflect on their own work and targets. The advantage of reflecting and correcting at the start of the lesson is that you may want students to set themselves a target based upon your marking for the lesson they are about to begin, and thus action that target as they proceed through the lesson.

# Build in time to REFLECT and CORRECT.

## Contextualise the lesson

One of the key aims of a starter should be to link up students' thinking. You want to ensure that they understand the journey: where you are coming from and where you are going to. Therefore, great starters will link previous lessons' work to future work – in essence, giving them the big picture. The start should either recap the previous lesson's work or introduce a new section of content or skill to be mastered.

## Set the pace and tone of the lesson

A purposeful and pacey starter can have a mesmerising effect on a class and drastically reduce the number of behaviour issues if delivered in the right way. As mentioned previously, the key is routine. Keeping your starters slick and speedy is a great way to engage the class from the outset and also reinforce the fact that your classroom is a place where there are high expectations and the learning is purposeful.

## Dialogue examples to support you

**'Picture this'**

'What would you see, hear, smell?'

'What's happening outside of the picture?'

**'Would you rather . . .?'/ 'What if . . .?'/ 'What happens next?'/Grandma went to market/Back to back/Just a minute**

'Use key words in your answer'.

'Use impressive words in your answer'.

'Prioritise your points'.

'What's the most important reason?'

**Reflect and Correct**

'You have five minutes to REFLECT and CORRECT; correct all your SPAG errors and write a target for today's lesson based upon feedback'.

'Swap your books and make sure your partner has corrected all their SPAG errors'.

'Susan, what is your target for today's lesson?'

'How do you think you can meet that target?'

### Contextualise the lesson

'How does this link to last lesson?'

'What do you think we will be learning about today?'

'What could we learn today that would be a good link to last lesson?'

'How could we develop that skill today?'

### Set the pace and tone

'You know what to do, the starter is on the board'.

'Books are on your desk, reflect and correct'.

'Get on with the challenge whilst I take the register'.

**Starters, in a nutshell**

- They are a significant feature to a successful outstanding lesson.

- They serve several purposes: They can help to manage behaviour, close the gap on students' understanding and fill in the gaps for students who were absent last lesson.

- They are an opportunity for students to reflect and correct their own work.

- They can create passion and enthusiasm for your subject matter.

- They set the pace and tone of the lesson.

**Figure 3.2**   Starters, in a nutshell

# 4

# Success criteria

## The pursuit of excellence

Establishing success criteria can often be the most time-consuming aspect of lesson planning, because it challenges us, as teachers, to carefully consider what we want the students to be able to achieve; therefore, it is the crux of any planning. It is obviously connected to your lesson objectives and learning question and, therefore, they need to be considered in tandem. It offers clarity to both student and teacher about what you are trying to accomplish, master and fulfil. Success criteria inform students of where they are on their learning journey, and illuminate what they need to do to move on to the next stage in their development. They help students to focus on the learning outcomes, and can give them a sense of autonomy to achieve their own goals. They inspire students to aim higher, motivate them to achieve their goals and provide a logical sequence for all students. Success criteria should be aimed right at the top of their ability. I often introduce this as 'I want this to be the best piece of work you have ever done', or 'If this were the best piece of work you had ever done, what would it include?' Using those simple sentences challenges the students to work at their highest level, engaging them to study the criteria to achieve in line with your highest expectations. It moves students away from mediocrity and encourages them to pursue excellence.

There are a few points to consider when writing success criteria:

- Be clear yourself what success looks like, in other words, know what you want from the students.

- Communicate this message clearly.

- Success criteria should increase the level of challenge for all students.

- Get students to discuss with you their understanding of the criteria. This minimises ambiguity and uncertainty, so that all students know exactly what is expected from them. To help you achieve this, write your criteria clearly in student-friendly language so that all students can access it.

- Show them what success looks like (if you want). A demonstration or a sample of model work can save valuable time, presenting a definitive example of what you want them to achieve and also what can be achieved by students in the same age group.

I add 'if you want' because there may be occasions when you want your students to be exceptionally creative and develop their own ideas and thus not have their creativity clouded by the work of others.

- Success criteria do not have to be constrained to one lesson or to one topic. If you really consider your criteria carefully, then, it can be applied to several lessons throughout the year and therefore reduce workload. For example, you may develop generic criteria for writing evaluations that can used for different year groups and different topics whenever you evaluate.

- Success criteria are all about getting students to aim higher and improve their work, rather than complete a number of tasks. For this reason, they should focus on knowledge development (key content of the subject), depth of understanding concepts or ideas (making sure they really understand what you have taught them) or developing skills (whether they be practical skills, subject-specific skills or skills connected to speaking, reading or writing).

Success criteria do not have to be constrained to one subject; they could be used across the school to help to develop consistency of approach. An example of success criteria that

**Table 4.1** Success criteria

| Standard | Paragraphs | Vocabulary/key words | Spelling, punctuation and grammar |
|---|---|---|---|
| | *Skill: How to structure a piece of written work* | *Knowledge: To know specialist terms used in the subject or to know the meanings of words to make the text more interesting.* | *Understanding: To understand when to use capital letters and where to use punctuation marks.* |
| Mastery/enhanced | I construct engaging paragraphs. New paragraphs begin whenever I change Time, Place, Topic or Person (TIPTOP). I use a wide range of connectives to link ideas together. | I use impressive vocabulary throughout to develop my points and engage the reader. I use a wide range of key terms appropriately within my written work. | My spelling punctuation and grammar are correct throughout. |
| Secure | I use paragraphs in my work to make my writing clearer for the reader. I use some connectives to link ideas together. | I use vocabulary suited to the task and use a number of key terms within my work. | Generally my SPAG is correct throughout. I make slight errors with more difficult words and key terms. |
| Developing | My work lacks structure and I need to use more connectives in my work to link ideas together. | I am beginning to use a wider vocabulary to engage the reader and I use some key words. | I can spell commonly used words; however, there are some mistakes within my work. |

could be used across the curriculum are those for extended writing. For the purpose of the example, I have added a row highlighted in italics to demonstrate how to incorporate skills, knowledge and understanding into a success criteria grid. However, this does not necessarily need to be shared with the students.

The advantage of these criteria is that they can be used time and time again whenever you require the students to produce a piece of extended writing. The students begin to recognise what is required to achieve at a higher level, and for the teacher it is a set of criteria to mark against and on which to provide feedback. The advantage of using the same criteria consistently either within your subject or across the school is that they become engrained in the students' practice. By continuous and consistent repetition of the standards, students develop a sense of automaticity to their writing: They instinctively come to know that an excellent piece of work will contain a distinct structure, supported by paragraphs, including impressive and specialist vocabulary and faultless spelling, punctuation and grammar. But the criteria do not have to stop there. You could ask the students to devise another column. 'What else could you include to show you have mastered this topic'? This engages students to think more deeply about what success would look like and consider what their best work would include.

Table 4.2 shows another example for Science.

Success criteria do not always need to be designed by the teacher; some of the best criteria I have used have been developed by the students themselves. Take the onus off yourself and pass it to the students – get them to do the work for you. With a bit of guidance, the outcome can be far better than what you thought possible. This can be achieved by asking the following questions:

'What would a top grade/score piece of work include?'

'Can we spilt that list up into categories?'

'Can we come up with a few examples of what a top piece of work would include?'

'How could we prioritise the skills?'

'What would an expert include in this work?'

Success criteria do not always have to be attached to a level, grade or score – in some cases, it may be a simple checklist for students to follow so that they are aware of what to include, and if they include all the relevant points then their work will be successful. That's not to say that this list should not be challenging for all students. Ian Smith, author of *Sharing Learning Intentions* (2007), suggests using the following stems to help you write success criteria that challenge all students and demand deeper thinking.

**I can . . .**

- Give explanations of . . .

- Identify ways to . . .

- Suggest reasons for . . .

**Table 4.2** Success criteria for science

| Standard | Thinking like a scientist. | | | |
|---|---|---|---|---|
| Mastery/enhanced | I can link ideas when explaining processes and concepts. | I critically evaluate ideas and models by identifying good and bad points. | I can use selective and complex evidence to support or deny scientific ideas. | I can write like a scientist using specialist terms, clear explanations and detailed conclusions. |
| Secure | I can link ideas when describing processes and concepts. | I can suggest solutions to problems and answer scientific problems. | I can use evidence to support or deny scientific ideas. | I write like a scientist, using some specialist terms, and I include an explanation and a conclusion. |
| Developing | I can use scientific ideas when describing simple processes. | I can use simple models to describe scientific ideas. | I can begin to use straightforward evidence to support or deny scientific ideas. | I use some specialist terms and my written work shows structure. |

- Predict that . . .
- Give examples of . . .
- Describe . . .
- Plan . . .
- Present . . .
- Determine the key points for . . .
- Make links between . . .
- Interpret . . .
- Show ways of . . .
- Decide . . .
- Explain that/what/how/why . . .

These stems can be developed by the students so they take ownership of their own learning and progress.

## How to use success criteria in the lesson

Once you have produced your success criteria, use them. This may sound obvious, but I have observed many lessons where the criteria are flashed up on a presentation slide for

30 seconds and then taken down, forgotten or referred to only at the end of the lesson. As with most guides, they should be continually consulted to ensure progress is being made. This does not mean stopping the lesson every five minutes to discuss progress, but that the students to refer to it themselves so as not to disturb the flow of the lesson or their learning. The criteria are for them to use to check their progress as they move along their learning continuum. Within the lesson, you may want a quick pit stop to confirm that students are engaging with the criteria. Ask students to review their own work and their peer's progress. How closely matched are they to the criteria? What do they need to do to improve? Students can set each other targets to improve using the specific criteria. Getting the students to reflect on what they have produced so far can create an opportunity to correct their course and stay on track to successfully produce their 'best' work.

## Success criteria are the map to achievement along the learning journey.

Plenaries to lessons provide the ideal opportunity for students to reflect on how well their work matches the success criteria. This can be done in a number of ways as discussed in the plenary section; however, one quick technique I use that I find very powerful is to ask the students where they are on the 'learning ruler'. I have a metre stick that I hold up and run my finger along, and I ask individual students to say 'stop' where they feel they are on the learning ruler. One end of the ruler is 'I don't understand at all' (0%) and the other end is 'I've totally mastered it' (100%). Students will often ask me to stop at around the 70–80% (cm) point. It is the next question that makes all the difference. I then ask, 'OK. You're here at about 70%. What can you do to get to here, 100%?' The responses are amazing! Students wisely considering and reflecting on their learning, coming up with their own targets for improvement without being told I then just add, 'Go on then, do it'.

## Dialogue examples to support you

Whilst planning the lesson, consider the following questions:

'What do I want the students to know or understand by the end of this lesson OR which skills do I want them to have mastered by the end of the lesson?'

'What does mastery look like, how will I know they have mastered the skill, concept or content?'

'How will the students demonstrate what they have learned?'

Within the classroom, the following statements and questions may help to deliver the outcomes you want:

'Read the criteria carefully. Are there any words you don't understand?'

'What does this criteria mean? Susan, can you put that into your own words?'

'What will the best work include?'

'I want this to be the best piece of work you have ever done at this school. What will you do to make sure this is your best?'

'Remember to refer to the criteria. They are your guide to success and excellence.'

'What could you add to make it even better?'

'Do you think you have now mastered . . . How do we/you know?'

---

**Success criteria, in a nutshell**

- Be clear about what success looks like.

- Pursue excellence. Set the bar high, Don't accept mediocrity.

- Ensure all students know what you are after.

- Use the criteria, either as self, peer or teacher assessment.

- Make sure the feedback incorporates the points of the criteria.

**Figure 4.1**   Success criteria, in a nutshell

# 5

# Practice makes progress

## How to build resilience and G.R.I.T.

In the previous chapter, you read about success criteria and pursuing excellence, setting the bar high and not accepting mediocrity. That all sounds fine, but what happens when the students don't achieve this lofty standard? How can we stop students from giving up and how can we build resilience and grit?

The first point I would like to make is that there has be to be a combination of challenges, some of which the student can achieve with sound application, and some of which push the very boundaries of their comfort zone and may appear unattainable. I don't believe that subjecting a student to lesson after lesson of failure, never attaining success, is of any use to student or teacher, and it inevitably damages the student's passion for learning your subject. Thus, students must be able to achieve their goals in some lessons, thereby building the confidence within your subject that they can draw upon when times get tough.

With the challenges you set at the very highest level, it is inevitable that not all students will be able to achieve the standard first time. So the big questions are: 'How do you help students to manage failure?' and 'How can you build resilience and grit so that students come back fighting time and time again and don't just give up?'

There is a wide range of psychological theory and conjecture related to this topic and I do not profess to know all the scientific working of the brain when faced with challenge and dealing with failure. What I can offer is my own views of the issue based upon research and my own experiences within the classroom.

In her book, *Mindset: How You Can Fulfil Your Potential* (2012), Carol Dweck discusses the mindsets of students when faced with a challenge. She recognises that some students have a fixed view of their intelligence. They have the view that they were born this way, and that no matter how much they try, they will never be able to accomplish a particular task because they are not clever enough. These students have a 'fixed mindset' and demonstrate self-defeating behaviours, saying things such as:

'I can't do this'

'I'm no good at these things'

'I've never had a good memory'

Her research also shows that some students have a 'growth mindset'. They believe they can improve their performance with hard work and effort and they recognise that failing once does not limit what they can achieve; they must learn from the mistakes and try again. 'Growth mindset' students say things like:

'I need to try that again'

'Next time I'll try harder'

'I've got to figure this out'

'I think I've almost got it'

With any activity you present to your students, you are likely to display the two mindsets, and it is tuning in to their responses that will guide you as to how to respond and help students to engage once more with the challenge. It's important to recognise how students react when faced with challenges. Those with fixed mindsets may react in several ways:

1) **Frustration**: These students may push the book away, throw down the pen, put their heads on desks and say things such as:

   'This is too hard'

   'I can't do this'

   'I give up'

2) **Aggressive disengagement:** These students may swear, become agitated and need to walk away from the desk. They may say things like:

   'I'm not doing this anymore'

   'This is crap'

   'What's the point in this?'

3) **Submissive:** They believe that they simply can't do it. They may go unnoticed for a time, sitting quietly, but not engaging with the activity, perhaps swinging back on a chair to psychologically distance themselves from the work. When you speak to them, they say things like:

   'I was waiting for you to tell me the answer'

   'I just don't get it'

   'I didn't understand what I had to do so I was just waiting' (possibly for the lightning bolt!)

# So how do we get the disengaged to engage?

The answer is to instil in your students the understanding that learning is all about making progress, and how do you achieve progress? You practise. It's the recognition that they, as with all of us, are on a learning curve and that learning never stops. Talking to disengaged students is the ideal time to share your own life experiences, explaining how you are still learning how to develop your own teaching practice and how yourself are not the finished article. Perhaps sharing an anecdote about how you overcame failure or dealt with a difficult challenge would be helpful. Understanding that failure and difficulty are fundamental to any success you and the students will achieve is key to building G.R.I.T. Therefore, a low score or grade on a snapshot test or exam becomes a stepping stone to better things rather than an insurmountable barrier to success.

## G.R.I.T.

We all suffer setbacks, disappointment and failures, and it is what we do next that matters most. Do we wallow in self-pity or do we show G.R.I.T.? The acronym is made up of the following four components:

**G – Growth:** The understanding that learning is a process and the ability to recognise that they are at a stage of development.

**R – Resilience:** The ability to recover from a setback or failure.

**I – Ingenuity:** Having the resourcefulness and initiative to solve problems and overcome challenges.

**T – Tenacity:** Having the ability to persist at a challenge until the desired outcome is attained. This is often referred to as 'stickability', the ability to stick at a task until you have achieved your goal.

## Strategies to create G.R.I.T.

1) **Explain RESPONSIBILITY:** The first key idea for students to grasp is that they are responsible for their own learning and thus their own success or failure. I endeavour to develop this approach within all my students. I continually refer to the need for them to take responsibility for their own learning and behaviour, and it is they who make the decisions on how they react to any challenge or instruction. When I first begin to prepare my exam classes for their final examinations, I remind them of the fact that they will achieve the grade they deserve. I remind them that I have taught them all the same set of skills and the same content and they have individually chosen their responses to my instructions, feedback and questions. They have either taken

on board my advice, asked questions to further their understanding and knowledge, acted on feedback and practised their subject-specific skills to achieve an outstanding grade – or they have not and therefore will not achieve the grade to which they aspire. They have had the same teacher, the same contact and the same opportunities, yet some will underachieve and others will thrive; the difference is that some students have accepted responsibility for their own learning.

The word *responsibility* is derived from two words, *response* and *ability* – in other words, the ability to respond positively to a given situation. How well students respond to feedback or failure is how they build G.R.I.T. Do they take it on the chin and learn from mistakes, or do they blame others, saying things such as, 'It's not my fault I failed; the exam paper was confusing' or 'I had the wrong pen; no wonder I messed up'. You build resilience by seeing failure as a learning opportunity – not as a nail in the coffin of success, not as a ceiling to all you can achieve, but rather as a stepping stone to achieving what you desire.

So how do we get students to accept responsibility? We tell them. Talk to them in a nonjudgement manner. Simply explain the facts. Tell them that they are responsible. It sounds daft, but many students have never been faced with the realisation that they will determine how well they will achieve. Students can be blinkered into thinking that success will be delivered for them and that there is a big safety net somewhere to scoop them up and provide for them. Welcome to the real world: You get out what you put in. Remind them of the consequences of their actions. Ask them, 'What do you think will happen if you fail your exams?' Again, I ask them this in an informal, nonjudgemental way, and then I don't speak. I wait for a response. I am always genuinely curious to hear their answer. It can give you fascinating insight into their thought process. I am often surprised by their short term thinking; they have often not considered what the likely outcome will be.

2) **Manage moments of truth:** Within every school day, the teachers and students are engaged in a number of 'moments of truth'. These are single moments when teachers and students have an opportunity to decide how they respond to any given situation. For example, the students who have just received a low grade or score in an exam: Do they blame the teacher and make excuses for the poor performance, or do they accept that they are accountable for their grades and recognise the fact that they must make improvements in the future if they are to experience success? Of course, as teachers we always want the second response, but it can be difficult for students to reflect in such a mature manner. It's important to recognise that we are dealing with children and young adults. Expecting them to respond in such a thoughtful and considered way is asking a lot; I know many adults who do not think in this way yet. However, this does not mean we shirk from the task but instead that we support students to respond in a positive way. One of the most common moments of truth that teachers face within the classroom will

be the student who 'can't do it', whether this be a particular skill/knowledge deficit, such as how to calculate the circumference of a circle in Maths, or learning new concepts and ideas such as the respiratory system in Science. How a student responds to failure is crucial to their short and long term achievement within the subject.

Teachers can help to manage student responses by asking the right questions. This is a key strategy to building G.R.I.T. because:

- Questions require answers.

- Answers demand thought.

- Thought creates decision.

- Decision inspires positive action.

Below are a number of questions that require students to reflect on their learning and inspire positive action:

- What strategies have you tried so far?

- What part are you struggling with the most?

- If you were in Science, how would you answer this question? (Helping students to recognise that may skills are transferable)

- On a scale of one to ten, where are you? What can we do to get you to ten?

- What progress have you made so far?

- What are your options?

- Have you solved a problem like this before?

- Break it down into steps: What can you do first?

3) **Sell them success:** When students have a negative mindset or have failed at a task, they can often become disengaged, disruptive and disheartened. In these situations, the onus is on us to sell them success, to get them to buy into the fact that if they stick with it and become more resilient then they will achieve their goals. Some students are quick to give up on challenges and themselves, and write them off as to too hard, too boring and pointless. By adopting the structure below you can help restore confidence and build self-esteem by securing success.

## Build a T.E.A.M

T: **Tune in:** Tune in to their response to the challenge: Are they frustrated, aggressive or submissive? Show understanding and empathy to their situation. You may say things such as:

I understand that you're frustrated . . .

I know you're angry you can't do it . . .

This is really tricky. I know you're finding it difficult . . .

Don't give up; you're going to solve it . . .

Don't worry; you are going to get this . . .

Remember: Learning is a process – you're not supposed to understand everything the first time.

**E: Explain:** Explain how you are going to support them, so they can solve the problem themselves:

I'm going to talk you through the process so you get it.

Watch how I do it, and I'm going to ask you some questions.

Let's break it down into steps.

I'm going to ask you some questions to help you understand . . .

**A: Advantages:** Outline the advantages of them sticking with it (tenacity) and remind them of past success:

Once you understand this, it will all fall into place.

The benefits are that you will then be able to . . .

The good thing is that you can then . . .

Get this and you can achieve fantastic grades/scores.

By learning this, you can improve your understanding of . . .

By learning this, you can improve you grade/score in . . .

Remember, you did something similar last week and you were great at that.

You understood . . . so I know you can do this.

You got a great score on the last test so you know you can do it.

**M: Monitor:** Monitor their response. Remember, you want a positive response; you don't want to walk away from them having made no impact, with the student still sitting there doing nothing. This last element should always be a question that will elicit a response. Ask the question and wait for an answer. Don't interrupt. Let them speak; you are trying to get them to come up with the solutions themselves, building that G.R.I.T. If the answer is a negative one, then go back to the advantages again and reinforce the positives of resilience.

How does that sound?

Is that OK with you?

What do you think of that?

Is that alright?

Shall we give it a go?

So a typical scenario may go something like this:

'Listen, I know you're frustrated. Let's look at it together and I know you will be able to do it. Remember, if you stick at it and you learn this, it will make a huge difference to your overall grade. So let's break it down into steps and I'll ask you some questions to help you understand. How does that sound?'

'I won't get it.'

'You will, because you understood how to do . . . And this is a similar process. So, shall we give it a go?'

'Alright, then.'

'Fantastic.'

4) **Praise the progress:** A foundation to building G.R.I.T. involves the type of feedback you give to students. Feedback is tackled in more depth in a later chapter, but a key principle is to praise the progress. This means praising the progress the student has made towards the final desired outcome rather than just the outcome of the activity. By recognising the efforts made by the student, we reinforce what we are trying to achieve, which in turn is building G.R.I.T. The danger of praising the outcome is that students can shrink their horizons to ensure they always receive praise. For example, if I constantly shower appreciation on student X for completing a lovely poster, why would they ever want to produce anything different/of a better standard? However, if I change my praise to 'What a fantastic effort – I think you've really shown progress today', then the student is far more inclined to want to replicate the processes that gained them that praise. After all, no matter what our age, we all like recognition for the effort we have made with a challenge.

5) **Use the power of YET:** In a TED talk Carol Dweck delivered in 2014, she spoke about the power of the word YET. She discussed a scenario in which students who had sat an exam and failed to meet the necessary criteria for a pass were given the feedback 'not yet' and how this had been a powerful tool to promote resilience. I, too, think this is hugely powerful word to use with students. It does not set a ceiling for students but promotes the idea that they are on a learning journey. It does not label or pigeonhole students (by saying or implying 'you are a C grade student' or 'a Level 5 student'), but

rather it illuminates the idea that they have not yet reached their potential. Below are two examples of how I use it within my classroom:

'I can't do this question, I don't understand.'

'You don't understand it *yet*, so let's break it down into parts and give it another go.'

'I'm never going to get an A.'

'You haven't got an A *yet*, so what can you do to improve your grade next time?'

The language we use with students can be incredibly powerful, especially at times of vulnerability, such as just after they have received a disappointing score on a test. Using 'yet' supports our goal to improve student performance by reminding them that their learning journey is not over; it is just at a stage along the way.

6)  **Practice makes progress:** We all know the adage 'practice makes perfect'. However, are we really always striving for perfection? By its very nature, perfection can rarely be achieved and is thus outside the grasp of many students. I'm not saying that it is not something to aim for – just that it is important to recognise that disheartening emotions can be created when students do not achieve it. Perfection is the outcome,

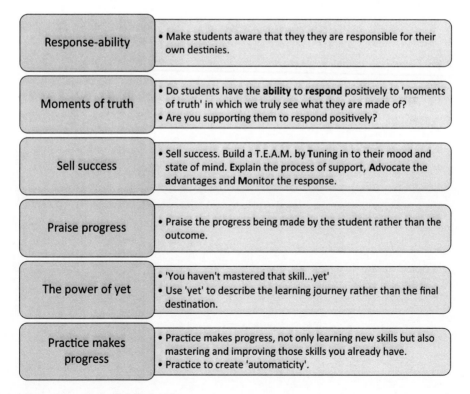

**Figure 5.1**   How to build G.R.I.T.

not the process; we should practise and model the process rather than an outcome. When we talk about practice, we unassumingly talk more about the progress made than about the final outcome. We may recount stories of how we practised a particular skill until we achieved success or describe how a famous footballer practises a particular drill until she can score wonder goals from thirty yards out. We must help students recognise that it is the progress aided by practice that is the most important aspect of learning, and that if we practise and make progress then the outcome will take care of itself.

---

**Practice makes progress, in a nutshell**

- Help students to respond positively to challenging situations and failures.

- Manage 'moments of truth' by asking considered questions.

- Sell them success by building a T.E.A.M.

- Praise progress, not just the final outcome.

- Respond to negative talk by using YET.

- Practice is the key to any progress.

**Figure 5.2**   Practice makes progress, in a nutshell.

# 6

# Differentiation

This term often appears to have an intangible element with many teachers finding it difficult to explain or achieve and having no real grasp of what good differentiation looks like in a classroom. Put simply, I believe that differentiation is about offering appropriate challenge to ALL students. ALL students are pushed to achieve their very best and support and scaffolding are provided to help them to achieve this.

The idea that this requires five different worksheets and that you have to greatly modify your teaching style is simply wrong. Of course, not all lessons can be fully differentiated; sometimes it's just necessary for the students to know specific content. That said, this is often an overlooked strand of excellent teaching, and if we want all our students to be successful, we must recognise that they are at different stages of their development and thus we must cater to their individual needs.

## Challenge choice

This technique allows the students to access your lesson at different levels. This could be matched to grade boundaries or success criteria previously shared with students. Students can then be guided to specific questions or they can challenge themselves and choose to answer more difficult questions. The different shades in Table 6.1 represent different levels of challenge for the students; the white questions are easiest and the darkest grey questions are hardest. You may wish to use random colours, such as yellow, blue, and green.

The benefit for the teacher is that the tasks can be linked to the levels or grades of the student. For the student, the benefits are ownership of their own learning, the opportunity to access the learning and the knowledge that they can challenge themselves to achieve and succeed.

## Case study: Geography

Having been taught the content of the course on flooding, the students are then presented with a newspaper article from a recent flood event. The teacher then presents the range of challenge choices shown in Table 6.1.

**Table 6.1**   Challenge choice

| Describe the photograph of the flood. | Explain the causes of the flood. | Prioritise the effects of the floods and justify your reasons. |
|---|---|---|
| List the effects of the flood. | Compare this flood to the flood in Bangladesh. | How could the flood problem be solved? |

This framework provides the teacher with a range of opportunities:

1) High ability students can answer the darkest grey questions, middle ability the medium grey questions and low ability the white.

2) Students can select the question they want to answer and challenge themselves.

3) The teacher can direct the students to answer at least one question from each colour.

4) Once students have answered their questions, they have to share their answers with another student so that they all collect the relevant information; the challenge is that each student must teach another the answer.

5) Appropriate targets can be set.

6) The questions can be matched to differentiated resources (for example, 'To answer the darkest grey questions, use the GCSE textbook').

7) Students can be grouped for support.

8) Some students can answer all the darkest grey questions; some students can be selected to answer a white question first before proceeding on to medium grey and then darkest grey.

## Differentiation is about offering appropriate challenge to ALL students.

This technique offers a plethora of possibilities. For example, you can offer just three questions or nine, and they can be exam questions or questions that the students generate themselves. You can tell the students which are the harder questions, or you can ask them to figure it out for themselves.

The question/verb stems are derived from Bloom's Taxonomy; they offer increasing levels of challenge to develop students' thinking and their understanding of a topic. Table 6.2 shows a sample of question/verb stems that could be used, crudely placed into three columns of challenge.

**Table 6.2** Question stems

| Low ability | Middle ability | High ability |
|---|---|---|
| Describe . . . | Explain . . . | Prioritise . . . |
| Label . . . | Outline . . . | How would you solve/improve . . . |
| Measure . . . | Discuss . . . | Can you predict . . . |
| Select . . . | Compare . . . | Justify . . . |
| Sketch . . . | Classify . . . | What would happen if . . . |
| Name . . . | Summarise . . . | How could you test . . . |
| Pick out . . . | What is the main idea about . . . | Can you offer an alternative . . . |
| Who, what, when, where, | What is the pattern of . . . | How would you measure/rate . . . |
| why . . . | Connect . . . | Why do you think . . . is not/is |
| Define . . . | Translate . . . | important . . . |
| List . . . | Can you link . . . | |
| Highlight . . . | | |

## Mount progress

Set up a number of work stations containing questions pitched at three different levels: questions to develop students' skills and knowledge, questions that will consolidate and secure students' understanding and questions that will allow them to demonstrate mastery of the subject or topic. The students can work their way around the classroom selecting questions from these three question stations. As the students complete each question, these can be marked and checked by the teacher, by a lead learner or by the students themselves as they refer to the mark scheme and self-assess their work. Once they have met the success criteria, they can then plot their progress on the 'progress board'. They write their name on a sticky note and stick it underneath the relevant criteria heading: developing, secure or enhanced/mastery. The students enjoy moving their names up the board, and the teacher can quickly see a visual picture of who is progressing well and who may be struggling in order to swiftly support them as needed. I use a mountain scene (Mount Progress) as a metaphor for climbing to success; I have seen colleagues who have a rocket in a solar system or a target board.

## Challenge questions

If you are faced with a student who has completed all the work to a standard you deem acceptable, 'challenge questions' are a fantastic device to develop that student's knowledge and understanding further. I have an envelope on my progress board containing a number of generic, open ended challenge questions that students can collect and answer at any point during the lesson once they have completed all their work. These questions often require higher level thinking and push the student on towards mastery. The questions can even be distributed towards the end of the lesson for students to answer as a plenary task. Below is a sample of some of the questions I use.

**Challenge Questions:**

- Design success criteria to judge whether somebody has progressed today.

- Write down six things you have learned today. Then order them in importance.

- Design a set of symbols to represent what you have learned during the lesson.

- Choose three key words we have used today and write their definitions.

- Write a short quiz based on today's lesson, then test your partner's knowledge.

- Draw a cartoon strip showing what you have learned during the lesson.

- Swap your work with somebody and assess it: What have they done well and what can they do to improve?

- Design a multiple choice quiz of ten questions to test the class.

- How could you improve your performance next lesson?

- What can you do now that you could not do at the start of the lesson?

## How can I support all students to achieve?

Some students may require additional support to answer the questions. This can be provided in a number of ways. Below are three key techniques that I believe provide the biggest impact.

1) **Sentence stems:** Give students examples of how to begin their writing or key connectives to use in their written work. Below are some examples:

*Sentence stems*

Firstly, secondly, finally . . .

Compared with . . .

Likewise . . .

To begin with . . .

With regard to . . .

In addition . . .

. . . therefore . . .

This caused . . .

As a result of . . .

For example . . .

2) **Lead learner:** Give one student the title of the lesson's lead learner; it is his or her responsibility to go around and make sure that students understand how to complete the challenges and to support them when necessary. The lead learner can also be the first port of call for any class questions, freeing the teacher up to work with individuals or groups who are struggling. The added responsibility of having to teach their peers is also a benefit for the lead learners, since having to teach requires a good knowledge and understanding of the topic and therefore creates appropriately high levels of challenge for that student, too.

I provide my lead learner with a lanyard and badge, but a sticker, hat or sash work just as well!

3) **Learning table:** Have a dedicated table or area where there is a range of resources to support students learning. You do not have to put out different resources for every lesson; simply provide a bank of materials for all lessons. This could include textbooks and revision guides from each key stage, key words cards with definitions, examples of excellent work and support sheets for structuring writing. The learning table, as well as offering constant support that does not involve you, helps to develop independent learning skills, the students' ability to take ownership of their learning and their skills in discovering answers for themselves.

## Dialogue examples to support you

Use these statements to help move your teaching on to the next level and engage students with differentiation.

'Today I want you to really challenge yourself; if you did a white question last time, today pick a medium grey question.'

'Susan, remember your target is to answer a darkest grey question today.'

'Those of you who picked a white question, come and work with me around this table.'

'Which questions were the hardest?' 'Why do you think that is the case?'

'Which key words do you think you will need to put into this answer?'

'What would the best answers to this question include?'

**Differentiation, in a nutshell**

- It's all about appropriate challenge, so that *all* students participate and achieve.

- Good differentiation allows *all* students to access the lesson.

- Keep your challenge choices open so that extension is developed in the students' work.

- Provide support and scaffolding for those groups of students that require it.

- Use prior assessments to match the students to the challenge choice.

**Figure 6.1**   Differentiation, in a nutshell.

# 7

# Questioning

Questioning is at the centre of all excellent teaching; it is what outstanding teachers spend most of their time doing. Questioning is an art and good questioning takes not only time to develop, but also a lot of practice and perseverance to hold out for the answer you want. The techniques below outline ideas to use when you want questioning to be the main focus at a particular point in the lesson and should be used when you want to really challenge students' thinking and deepen their understanding of a particular idea or concept. It does not mean that you should never take answers from students with their hands up or accept one word answers. All these techniques should be used as and when appropriate within a lesson.

The first key area that needs to be in place is the 'no passengers' approach. This means that all students participate and, therefore, it matters little whether or not students have their hands up. An important feature of excellent questioning is making sure that all students are involved and that there are no passengers in your lesson. Thus, all students have to concentrate and listen because they may have to answer a question. This technique aims to eliminate the attitude of 'well, he never asks me so I don't have to pay attention'. 'no passengers' requires that all students contribute a 'good' answer (i.e., an answer with which you are satisfied and not an 'I don't know' response). It is vital that you tackle the 'I don't know' response so that students are not allowed to get away with this as a standard response to avoid contributing to the lesson – or even because they are not confident in answering. We will look at ways to tackle this.

## 'No passengers'

Here are six killer ways to tackle students saying 'I don't know' and make sure everyone participates in your questioning.

1) **"Give it some thought. I'm coming back to you."** This gives the student thinking time; it may be that time is all that is required for the student to process the question and then come back with a response. It also allows time for the student to look in a book

or for a friend to whisper the answer to them. In my opinion, as long as it is not a test, it is acceptable for them to do this. The required outcome is that the student gives a 'good' answer to the question and feels successful at that moment. Your praise will help to build confidence, which will in turn promote more engagement and greater willingness to contribute further down the line. 'Give it some thought' instructs the student to consider their answer rather than shouting out the first idea that comes to mind; this should result in a more thoughtful and high quality answer. a key feature of 'Give it some thought. I'm coming back to you' is to make sure you remember to come back!

2) **'No rush; have a think.'** If nothing else, this statement reminds me, as the teacher, that students need time to process questions to be able to formulate an answer. Copious amounts of research have demonstrated that teachers, on average, allow only a 3-second response time before answering the question themselves or asking somebody else. A moment of silence is not to be feared but, in fact, encouraged as the pupil attempts the answer. Recent research states that teachers should wait 10–12 seconds for high order questions to be answered.

3) **'Susan, I'm going to ask you . . . in a minute so get thinking'.** Giving extra thinking time and pre-warning students that a question is on the way allows them to rehearse the answers in their heads or to find the answers in their books, if necessary. This is a good question stem for students with low confidence or those who rarely contribute answers, giving them the necessary time to prepare themselves.

4) **'What did . . . say?'** This question is posed to a student who has stated that he/she does not know the answer. The student then has the opportunity to experience success, develop listening skills and ultimately realise that he/she cannot opt out of giving an answer.

5) **'You've heard two answers; which one do you like the best?' 'Why?'** This again involves engaging with other students' responses. It requires students to use listening skills and a higher level of thinking to interpret and justify which answer they consider to be better and the reasons why.

6) **'Guess . . . '** Putting 'guess' at the beginning of a question makes students more comfortable in answering without worrying about making a mistake. Try it yourself, how do you feel in response to these two questions?:

'Name all the planets of the solar system.'

'Guess the names of the planets in the solar system.'

Did you feel more relaxed when considering answering the second version of the question than the first? The student is more at ease knowing that he/she can make a mistake; guessing is far more likely to elicit a response to a question than an 'I don't know', which is what we are trying to eradicate.

## Why it's important to say 'wrong'

Once all students are contributing and they have learned that they cannot get off the hook by simply saying 'I don't know', we need to move on to getting the answer you want. Too often when I observe colleagues, I see students giving the wrong answer and teachers replying with 'ooh you're close', or 'not quite', or 'I get what you're saying, but . . .' If the answer is wrong, it's wrong – tell them. I know this may sound heartless, and it is important to use common sense here. I would never think of telling the Year 7 student with low self-esteem who never says anything, 'Nope. Totally wrong.' There are ways around that, but the majority of students are far more resilient than we give them credit for and, after a few weeks of students being corrected, the climate in which it is acceptable to make mistakes becomes the norm. I believe that excellent teaching allows students to make mistakes so that they can learn from them and correct their own course.

So why is it important to tell students when they are wrong? Because it prevents misconceptions and confusion for all. If a student answers the question 'What temperature is the boiling point of water?' The answer comes back from the student '50°C', and you say, 'Yeah, close, nearly right' then some students, including the student who answered, will think that the answer could be 60°C or 40°C. Even if you do go on to say it is actually 100°C, the vague nature of your previous response has created confusion and doubt. Better to say, 'No, that's wrong; it's 100°C.' I appreciate that it does not come naturally to many teachers to say this – it may appear to damage confidence. However, we must simultaneously build resilience and create a culture in which is it acceptable and necessary to make mistakes in order to learn and make progress. This can only be achieved if students know what went wrong and what they need to do to improve or fix the problem.

## How to get *KILLER* answers

This involves setting answer standards (i.e., crafting the answer that you want). Getting the best answer out of students should translate to improved knowledge and a deeper understanding of the idea or concept you are teaching.

For ease of explanation, and to get students to engage with answer standards, I devised the acronym KILLER to explain killer answers.

K – Key words

I  – Impressive vocab

L – Linked ideas

L – Language

E – English as standard

R – Reflective

**Key words:** Promoting the use of key words within answers helps to develop the students' understanding of those terms by using them in a variety of contexts and also helps to build their oral and literacy skills. By using key terms often, students develop automaticity when talking about the topic. Using key words in speech can then translate into use in written work. Often on Parents' Evenings I hear colleagues saying, 'He can say it but he can't get it down on paper'. Yet improvements in oral answers convert to improvements in written answers.

**Impressive vocabulary:** The aim of this standard is for students to develop a more interesting and sophisticated vocabulary, which then translates to writing with more authority. This standard could be supported with a thesaurus. I have a class set of these readily available for students to use, and I have observed a significant improvement in the breadth of vocabulary used by the students within a short space of time. Practice is needed, but in time this becomes a common feature of the lesson. I also have a display of impressive vocabulary with the words and definitions that I encourage students to use in their writing.

**Linked ideas:** Students are encouraged to link ideas to develop the detail of their answers; thus, they move away from the practice of giving one word answers. This also helps to foster deeper thinking and problem solving. The students have to make links between ideas and concepts and therefore demonstrate a greater understanding of the topic or subject.

**Language:** This is really focused on the use of connectives to help students to link ideas together. These can be provided on a prompt card or word mat, and in time they become a common feature of students' dialogue.

**English:** The use of Standard English is of paramount importance within the classroom. If we are preparing our students for the world of work, we must instil high standards during their formative years in our classroom. It is therefore vital that slang and incorrect use of the English language is challenged and corrected. I believe we are doing the students a disservice if we repeatedly let errors go unchallenged and allow the incorrect use of Standard English.

**Reflective:** Considering the strengths and weaknesses of an answer gives the students the opportunity to improve on their answer and reflect on which parts are good and which areas need to be improved (for example, including a 'better' word or another linked idea).

## It is acceptable and necessary to make mistakes in order to progress.

## Dialogue examples to support you

Key words: 'Can you use the proper geographical/historical/scientific term?'

'That's a great use of key words'.

Impressive vocab: 'Can you give me a better word for . . .?'

'Can you give me an impressive vocab word in that sentence . . .?'

Linked ideas: 'And what could that lead to?'

'And then . . .?'

'Why?'

Language: 'Give me that answer in a full sentence'.

'Therefore . . .'

English: 'Use the proper standard English, thank you'.

'Like . . . or just . . . '

Reflective: 'What makes that a good answer?'

'Which key words did he/she use?'

'How could we improve that answer?'

'Could we add to that answer to make it even better?'

'What grade/score do you think that answer would get?'

---

### Questioning, in a nutshell

- Get all pupils to contribute to question and answer sessions.

- Don't allow passengers in your lesson.

- Allow time for pupils to think, consider and respond to your questions.

- Set answer standards and hold out for the answer you want before moving on.

- Don't be afraid to say 'That's wrong'.

**Figure 7.1**   Questioning, in a nutshell

# 8

# Modelling

*Modelling: Serving as an example to be imitated or compared.*

Modelling work is one of the most powerful techniques a teacher has to help to improve progress. It provides the scaffold to support students' learning and shows them a clear example of what you expect and what you want from them.

Modelling work isn't just about displays and saying, 'Isn't this good?' It should have depth, raise questions and inform the students on how they can be successful. The most success I have had with this technique is with GCSE and A level classes. By spending time focusing on each stage of the response process, students can taste success, knowing that they are crafting excellent exam answers, and they quickly buy into the system.

> ## If you want students to be successful, show them what success looks like.

## Stage 1: Command words

First, the exam question is dissected to reveal the command words. It is vital that all students know what you mean by the command words and time is spent initially explaining and defining them. Table 8.1 contains several of the most common command words in exam questions.

Begin by asking the students to identify the command words in the question and explaining what they mean. The two most common commands are *describe* and *explain*, and to tackle the confusion between these two terms, ask, 'What do we mean by describe?' Try to relate the question to the students – for example, let's DESCRIBE Jane's face: She has two blue eyes, a nose and a mouth. Now EXPLAIN Jane's face: Jane has blue eyes because she carries the blue eye genes of her mother and father and these genes have determined Jane's eye colour – that's why she has blue eyes. Her nose began forming as her cartilage and bone structure developed during the prenatal phase of her life; once she was born, her features have developed and changed with time. Students are quick to recognise the

**Table 8.1** Command words

| | | |
|---|---|---|
| **Describe** – This means 'say what you see'. Start by giving the main characteristics or features of something. "What does it look like?" | **Account for** – Give an explanation or reasons for something. This will require detail and explanation of why something has happened. | **Compare** – When you compare, you describe the similarities and differences of at least two things. |
| **Explain** – Give reasons why something happens. The points in the answer must be linked. | **Define** – Give the meaning of a word, phrase, idea or concept. | **Evaluate** – Pick out good and bad points and make judgements. |
| **Outline** – Provide a brief summary of the information; include the main points. | **Discuss** – This means you consider both sides of an argument (for and against), and come to a conclusion. You may need to EMPATHISE with different groups of people. | **Annotate** – This is more than just labelling. Add detail to a diagram or image. Add words that describe and/or explain the features. |

difference between the two terms. At this point, the teacher can ask for other words similar to the command word or ask students to write their own definitions of command words. Students then need to recognise key words in the questions and have a clear understanding of their meaning (for example, be able to answer the question, 'Give me another word for *effect?*'). The teacher can then write these synonyms around the word on the board (for example, *impact, result, consequence*). This then gives the students increased access to the question and improves their understanding of what they are being asked to do.

On the board, I may present an exam question and then ask the students a series of questions so that we can annotate the question; thus, all students develop a clear understanding about how to answer the question. See the example in Figure 8.1.

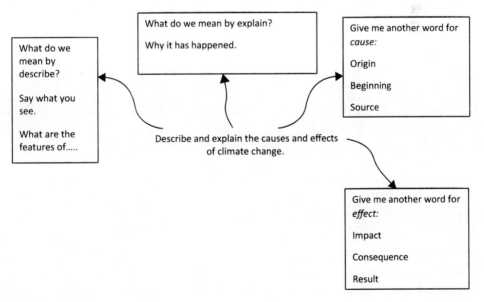

**Figure 8.1** Question annotations

## Stage 2: Success criteria

Having dissected and annotated the exam question, the next stage is to tell students what the best answers will include. These are the success criteria that allow students to understand what is needed to be successful. The criteria can be referred to throughout the lesson; bringing students back to look at these is good practice because it reminds them of what they need to include in order to gain a good grade or score. There are several options available to the teacher at this stage: You can write your own success criteria describing what you want students to include in their work, you can use the exam board's mark scheme or you can work in collaboration with the students and together write the success criteria so that the students take real ownership of the process. All three have their own merits, and you can use a variety of these techniques throughout the year.

Table 8.2 is an example of a success criteria grid that I use (amended from the AQA Geography A specification).

**Table 8.2** Success criteria

|  | Level 1: Basic 1–3 Marks | Level 2: Clear 4–6 Marks | Level 3: Detailed 7–8 Marks |
|---|---|---|---|
| **Knowledge** | Basic information. | Accurate information. | Accurate information linked to the content of the question. |
| **Understanding** | Simple understanding. | Clear understanding. | Detailed understanding, supported by relevant evidence and examples. |
| **Organisation** | Little organisation, few links, little or no detail, uses a limited range of specialist terms. | Organised answer, with some links, occasional detail/ examples. Good use of specialist terms. | Well organised, details, links shown and the inter-relationship between factors. Clear expression of ideas in a logical form. Uses a wide range of specialist terms. |
| **Spelling, punctuation and grammar** | Reasonable accuracy in the use of SPAG. | Considerable accuracy in the use of SPAG. | Accurate use of SPAG. |

## Stage 3: Content and key words

Through student participation and questioning, you are trying to scaffold an excellent answer for the students. This can be achieved by breaking down their response into paragraphs or points. Ask the students, "What would the best answers include?" This question challenges them to consider attaining above and beyond what they may think they can achieve. If they have only ever achieved a low grade, they may think the top grades are beyond their reach, but this question allows them to realise that they can achieve at the very top level if they spend time reflecting on what makes an excellent answer.

'What would you want to include in paragraph one?'

'Which key words would you need to include to achieve an A grade?'

'What would an excellent conclusion incorporate?'

All of these questions require the students to stop and consider their answers rather than put pen to paper straight away. Writing these on the board or asking students to write them down will help them to plan their response. Getting them to reflect on their responses and plan their answers can have huge gain margins when it comes to their examination performance.

## Stage 4: Appropriate challenge / differentiation

This is the point at which you introduce support, depending on the composition of your class. The support offered may be of various types – for example, sentence stems or a writing frame for the low ability, translated instruction sheet or key words sheet for EAL students. Word mats are a very useful support to help all students to structure their writing. Starters and connectives mats have been a valuable tool for me and many colleagues for students from Years 7 to 13. It helps them to use more sophisticated language, incorporate impressive vocabulary and link ideas together.

The open ended nature of the writing task will allow high ability students to write with expansion. However, to drive them on further and to truly challenge them, prompt them to consider their responses – prioritising their points and offering solutions to the problem or issue – or challenge them to write their own mark scheme.

## Stage 5: The writing process

For students to prosper, they must have a clear sense of direction, and we can provide the steps to success. Outlining and reminding students of the necessary procedures will guide them with their writing, ensuring that they stay on track throughout the writing process. At intervals throughout the lesson, you can stop the class to share good practice and model the good work so far. A visualiser/webcam connected to a computer is a handy tool to showcase students' work (asking the student to read out his/her work is a more-than-acceptable substitute). I walk around the class and read students' work. Having told a particular student that their work is good, I then place it under the visualiser/webcam and ask the class to read the work. I then ask the following questions:

'What's good about this piece of work?'

'Which key words or terms have been used?'

'What could they add to make it better?'

We discuss the features of the text that makes it successful and what may be added to improve it. It is often the students themselves who recognise in their own work what they can add to make it better. Having discussed what makes the work so good, I then tell the students to employ the same techniques. There is a range of other subject-specific questions that you can ask, but I find these three questions help to steer the whole class on to greater success.

# Stage 6: Peer and self-assessment

Once students have completed their answers to my satisfaction, I then ask them to assess their own work or that of a peer. I refer back to the success criteria, reminding them of what we said the best answers would include. Then, using this framework, I ask students to assess the work. One technique I use is to get the students to underline key words that they have used or connectives from the connectives word mat. I often introduce this task as a competition. Before anyone has started writing, I challenge the class to use the most connectives and key words they can; the person who includes the most wins a prize. Not to be sexist, but this extrinsic motivation works wonders with my low ability boys. Obviously, there may be subject-specific information that you want the students to highlight – for example, where they have used a simile or where they have used a scientific phrase. The point is for them to begin to recognise in their own and others' work the elements needed to be successful within the subject.

Examples of how peer and self-assessment can be used within subjects:

- Maths: Evaluations, conclusions and written instructions

- Technology: Evaluations

- Science: Write-up of experiments, long response questions in GCSE and A level examinations

- MFL: Extended writing opportunities

- Geography: Extended writing opportunities and exam responses at GCSE and A level

- History: Extended writing opportunities and exam responses at GCSE and A level

- RE: Extended writing opportunities and exam responses at GCSE and A level

## Dialogue examples to support you

'Which are the command words in this question?'

'Give me another word for . . .'

'Write your own definition of . . .'

'What would the best answers include?'

'What would you want to include in paragraph one?'

'Which key words would you need to include to achieve an A grade?'

'What would an excellent conclusion incorporate?'

'What's good about this piece of work?'

'Which key words or terms have they used?'

'What could they add to make it better?'

### Modelling, in a nutshell

- It's all about showing the students what the steps leading to success look like.

- Make sure they know what the question is really asking them.

- Support and scaffold so that they can craft excellent answers.

- Showcase the best work and let students see what they can achieve.

**Figure 8.2**   Modelling, in a nutshell

# 9

# Moving away from modelling

## How to create independence

Modelling work and good practice can be a key process to any learning within a lesson, allowing students to access the learning and gain success. It is vital that the support and scaffold is in place for students so that they are fully aware of what success looks like, how success can be measured and the necessary steps to gaining success. However, as the students develop the skills, knowledge and understanding of how to perform at their best, it is important to then begin to remove the support, giving them the chance to excel and discover for themselves. In other words, it's time for the stabilisers to come off! This can be a nerve-wracking time for both students and teacher: The students are given the freedom to discover and develop on their own, and for the teacher it's time to relinquish control and step back to see if the students can cut it in the real world, so to speak. This does not mean that you totally stop teaching; it means that you act more as a coach to the students' learning. The teacher then works to help students to develop their own clear questions for study, set a criteria for quality, plan for research and select an appropriate method of presentation and review.

From a teacher's point of view, you need to be clear about what you are trying to achieve and what you think success looks like. What do you want the students to know or be able to do at the end of the lesson, programme of study or learning episode? This is often a blend of subject content, deeper understanding of a concept or idea and subject-specific skills.

As the modern world changes rapidly and puts increasing pressure on the performance of students, we are increasingly hearing from leading figures in industry who say that schools are not providing workers of the future and that too many recent graduates lack the skills needed in the modern workplace. Creating independence does, therefore, not only develop subject-specific knowledge, understanding and skills, but also develops the necessary skills to enable students to be successful in later life. Independent learning provides the assortment of personal resources to allow students to thrive, including how to work with initiative, how to solve problems, how to transfer skills and how to be powerful learners. It is by developing these personal attributes that students become outstanding 21st-century learners and successful in later life. So when setting about creating independent work, it is important to consider that it is not only the aim to identify and improve key areas of learning for each of the students, but also to expand their capacities to learn and develop traits that will support them throughout their lives.

Independent learning, for many teachers, is like the holy grail of teaching: the idealistic utopia where all students want to learn and they merrily go about their business in lessons. The ideal scenario would be that you could walk into a class and say, 'Ok team, you all know what you're doing, you all know the aims and what you need to do to be successful, so off you go and I'm here if you need any help'. That idea can seem like a dream at times, but by employing some set procedures, we can increase the likelihood of making it happen in our classrooms.

## Stage 1: Have a clear starting point: Developing the learning question

At this stage, it is important to diagnose the students' learning needs, ensure students see the point of the learning and set out clear goals.

Learning needs can be diagnosed in two ways: student led or teacher led.

## Student led

The learning question could be established through a class discussion, either at the start, middle or end of a topic, by asking the following questions:

What would you like to learn about during this topic?

What do you already know about this topic?

What questions do you have about this topic?

Which parts have you struggled with?

What do you still not understand about this topic?

Look back at your previous tests/feedback. What do you need to work on?

The advantage of using this method is that it is totally student centred and reflective. Students are challenged to identify their own learning needs, which can help with motivation during the learning process. The disadvantage is that at this stage, as the teacher, you have little control of what the students are distinguishing as a learning need. This may greatly differ from your own thoughts or assessment. Therefore, it may be necessary to intervene to jointly ascertain a need.

## Teacher led

Learning needs may present themselves through previous assessments. However, this comes with a health warning: Assessments or tests will need to be dissected to discover the true issues for the student. It is important to note, for example, that two students who have identical scores of 10 out of 20 on a test may have widely differing strengths and weaknesses within that subject. Student X may have been excellent in the short response questions on topic one but weak on the longer questions on topic two, whilst student Y may have scored poorly on topic one and well on topic two (i.e., the same overall score was achieved but very different learning needs identified). It is vital that both student and teacher collaborate to improve the performance in those identified areas rather than a wide sweeping target being set to improve all areas. The advantage for the teacher is that you are able to steer the support for students to the specific learning needs they have identified. Also, this level of support may be necessary for weaker students who struggle to pinpoint a particular area to develop. The disadvantage is that students may feel they have little say in what they want to work on, taking away the autonomy we are striving to create. The best way to overcome this is through negotiation, discussing possible options and allowing the student to choose. Thus, they maintain autonomy whilst getting directed support from the teacher.

The teacher then works to help students to develop their own clear question for study, remembering that this must be matched to the identified aims. This could be whittled down to three to five questions that the individual student or class can then opt into. You may want to group students together to work on study questions collaboratively or you may want

**Table 9.1**   Differentiated study question stems

| Standard | Question stems | Key words |
|---|---|---|
| **Knowledge and comprehension** | Who, what, when, where, why?<br>How?<br>Describe . . .<br>Write in your own words . . .<br>What are the main ideas of . . . | Define<br>Explain<br>Discuss<br>Research<br>Outline |
| **Application and analysis** | Write a case study based on . . .<br>How does . . . compare/contrast with . . .?<br>What is the evidence for . . .?<br>Design a diagram/webpage/map to represent . . . | Demonstrate<br>Give an example<br>Investigate<br>Categorise<br>Report<br>Analyse |
| **Synthesis and evaluation** | Can you predict . . .?<br>Design a . . . to . . .?<br>What would happen if . . .?<br>What do you think is the most important . . .?<br>Do you agree that . . . Justify your answer . . .<br>What criteria would you use to . . . | Justify<br>Prioritise<br>Appraise<br>Improve<br>Conclude<br>Select<br>Assess |

*(Adapted from Bloom's Taxonomy)*

to differentiate the study questions, guiding certain students to certain study areas that you know they need to work on – or in which they will be successful and build confidence.

## Stage 2: Success criteria

This is the benchmark by which both you and the student will evaluate success. It sets the parameters within which to work and offers clarity to the investigation, enquiry or project. To create true independence, the student must design the success criteria; this develops higher orders of thinking than when students are told what they need to do. As with all things, students get better at considering what success looks like with practice; however, at an early stage support and guidance may be necessary. This can be offered by using a generic criteria. This may be an exam mark scheme or level descriptor. You may ask the class to discuss and design a set of criteria all together.

**Table 9.2**   Example of a generic criteria for project-based work

| Standard | Research question | Success criteria | Research | Presentation | Literacy | Numeracy |
|---|---|---|---|---|---|---|
| Mastery/ enhanced | I created my own research questions and selected the most appropriate one to investigate. | I designed and created my own success criteria. | I used a range of research methods and information sources with confidence, including textbooks, ICT and articles. | I used my research to write and produce my own work. I referenced all my work and was aware of bias from websites. | My spelling, punctuation and grammar are correct throughout. | All calculations are correct with workings out. Graphs and diagrams are accurately drawn and fully labelled using the correct axis and units. |
| Secure | I created my own research questions and, with help, chose the best one to investigate. | I used the model and other people's examples to help me write my own success criteria. | I used a limited range of research methods with guidance. | I produced my own work based upon my research. | Generally my SPAG is correct throughout. I make slight errors with more difficult words and key terms. | Calculations are correct but not all working out is shown. Graphs are well drawn and labelled. |
| Developing | I had help to write and develop my research question. | I had help to write my success criteria. | I was guided as to which books and websites to use. | I created my presentation with some guidance and assistance. | I can spell commonly used words; however, there are some mistakes within my work. | I was supported to complete calculations, and I needed guidance to draw graphs and diagrams accurately. |

## Stage 3: Planning

For some students, the idea of independence creates a sense of freedom and flexibility, a free licence to discover and flourish unburdened by the constraints of the teacher. For others, it is a daunting and foreboding task, filled with peril and potential ridicule. And then there are students who fall between those two extremes. Whatever students' mindsets, as teachers we are there to support and challenge so that all achieve a desired outcome. Along that continuum, we need to use our professional judgement as to those students we can leave alone to thrive and those who will need extra guidance. Below are a few key points that can help you achieve success for all.

## Setting goals

Having created your learning question, it is essential to have clear goals for how you will answer it. It is the ability to set meaningful goals and an associated action plan for their accomplishment that is one of the most important aspects that determines whether a student is successful or not.

**How to make SMART targets smarter:** This idea is adapted from an article by Joanne Miles. (/joannemilesconsulting.wordpress.com) She makes reference to the fact that the notion of SMART targets (specific, measurable, achievable and realistic) is now out of date for our 21st-century learners. Instead, we should be considering SMART as the following:

Stretching: Targets must challenge our students enough to make sure that they are engaged and stimulated to discover the answers.

Motivating: Linked clearly to the wider learning process and the ultimate goals of our students. Connect the learning to their life. For example, independent work will develop those skills that the working world is crying out for: initiative, research skills, communication skills and resourcefulness. If you guide them to independent work, not only will it help the students to achieve a higher grade/score, but it will give them the skills necessary to be successful in later life.

Actual: The target needs to be something the student can actually achieve. It needs to be personal to the student and realistic. For example, 'I will print off and highlight one article'.

Reviewed: The students work needs to be reviewed continually along the way. This could include self, peer, a one-to-one discussion with the teacher or marking for progress.

Talked about: Whether this is in pairs, in groups, or part of a class discussion, promoting a learning dialogue can help to remedy any problems encountered by the students. It also provides a useful barometer for the teacher to get a sense of how the class is progressing and where the issues may be that require additional support.

## Steps

The final outcome or finished project can appear a long way off and unattainable, so rather than concentrate on the final product, break it down into smaller manageable steps that collectively will give success and the desired outcome. It is the accumulation of these small incremental steps that will produce the final goal. Model this with the students and share anecdotes. Model this with the students and share anecdotes. Help them to realise that Van Gogh didn't paint the 'Sunflowers' in an couple of hours, Einstein didn't come up with the theory of relativity in an afternoon, Pele didn't become world class after one kick about with friends it was the culmination of hours of work and dedication. Reinforce the idea that they just need to concentrate on one task at a time rather than producing the final piece of work. Model 'steps' for them: If the final aim is a cup of tea, then this is broken down into the following steps:

1) Pour water into the kettle.

2) Turn the kettle on.

3) Add tea bag to a mug.

4) Pour boiling water into mug.

5) Stir.

6) Add sugar and milk.

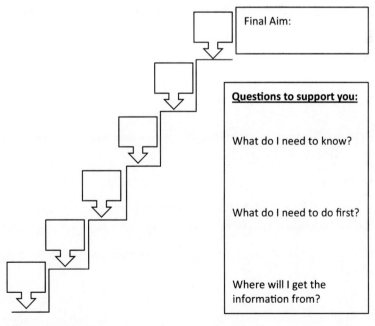

**Figure 9.1**   Planning sheet

You get the idea.

As the teacher, your role is often to ask questions that get students thinking about how they will achieve their goals and what the necessary steps are to get there. Their thoughts about the steps may highlight where they need support or what resources they need along the way.

# Stage 4: Research/activity

This is the stage that is generally the most disorganised and messy phase of the learning. As the teacher assuming the coaching role, you may need to offer guidance and support for this stage. If you just tell the students to go off and investigate their own research question, in a lot of cases you will end with a mix of weird and wonderful information, most of which has been copied and pasted into a presentation.

Great coaching is about asking questions and letting your students find the answers themselves. It's about students taking ownership of their own learning and achievements and becoming autonomous learners. So, instead of giving them a textbook and stating that all the information they need to answer their research question is on pages 25–30, instead you can ask them, 'Where do you think you could find the answers to your question?' 'How reliable do you think that source material will be?' 'What equipment do you think you would need for this experiment?' At this point, for some subjects you can introduce the idea of a learning log, a record of their learning journey. It records what source materials they have used, websites visited, time spent on each task, their assessment of how effective their research methods have been and their critique of sources on their reliability and usefulness. This allows students to chart their own progress and alter course if required.

## Navigating Research

If you want your students to become excellent researchers, they need to learn to be concise, controlled and efficient. Make sure they understand the following points:

- They must keep in mind what they are researching and why they are researching it. Is their research relevant to the question?

- They must recognise bias or propaganda by critiquing their sources.

- They must be selective with their research; some of their work may be irrelevant and they must be prepared to disregard some sources and some of their own notes.

- They cannot copy and paste; they must use the research to create their own work and opinions.

- They must periodically refer back to the research question. Are they still on course?

These skills can be modelled by you first, and very quickly the students will learn to become more effective and efficient researchers. The following ideas may seem basic techniques, but they have saved me a lot of time in past lessons, preventing me from having to answer the same questions time and time again. I start by demonstrating how to use a textbook, how to use the index and look up the relevant words and associated words and how to find them within a book. Simple, I know, but it does stop the constant questions of 'What page is . . . on?' As if I'm some textbook wizard!

Newspapers can be a fantastic source of information and can often provide different viewpoints of the same issues – a gold mine of information if you are comparing views or investigating conflicting arguments. I discuss the format and conventions of newspapers: Bold headlines are there to grab the readers' interest, the first paragraph is designed to give the key points of the story and the following paragraphs detail the specifics. I explain to the students that newspapers often write with bias, what we mean by bias, how to spot bias and why people write with bias.

The internet will be the first port of call for most students. Demonstrate how to use the internet efficiently. I model the difference between typing in a vague term such as 'volcanoes' compared to searching 'The causes of the 1994 eruption of Mt Etna'. These create vastly different websites to investigate. Getting students to use the internet concisely and efficiently is the aim, but wasting time looking at irrelevant sites or links to other stories can be a major stumbling block. The key is to set strict parameters: You may want to state specific time boundaries within lessons (for example, 'You have 30 minutes in today's lessons to produce two A4 pages with three pictures'). The benefit of this instruction is that it creates a sense of urgency for the students and also challenges them to prioritise their information, making them think, 'What are my three best pictures?' 'Do I need all this information or is a lot of it irrelevant?'

## Flipped classroom and homework

The concept of the flipped classroom is attributed to the Harvard Professor Eric Masur, who first developed the idea to move information transfer to outside of the classroom. This was later developed by two science teachers named Jonathan Bergmann and Aaron Sams, who saw that rather than lecture to students during tutorials, they could coach students on what they had learned at home. The premise is that the class-based activities and homework are reversed, thus 'flipping' the learning. Students can access online tutorials, lessons and electronic resources at home to learn new content or skills, and then understanding and consolidation of information is developed within the classroom. This idea or an adaption of this idea can be employed when working independently on a project.

In an ideal world, I would produce a number of video clips explaining the different concepts and ideas we are studying. To accompany this, I would have a number of online presentations to support the students' learning, with various resources and activities to complete that challenge them to develop their learning. However, in the real world, it would take me forever to produce the necessary resources. Therefore, delegate! One approach is to get the students to produce the resources for you. This could be the project material on which they are currently working. Then simply save their work so it is ready to support other students the following year or to model good practice.

Whether it is flipped learning or homework that you are setting, students must use it to support their knowledge and understanding in order to help them answer their learning questions. For independence, they should be setting their own goals for what they are trying to achieve in their homework, but these goals should then be used within lesson time to embellish their work.

## Stage 5: Methods of presentation

The subject you teach and your confidence with different presentational techniques will influence how you want your students to present their final pieces of work. Obviously, to encourage independence, the students should select their own methods of presentation; however, you may need to offer guidance if you require a particular style. Below are a few ideas and suggestions.

### Learning logs

These are personalised learning resources created by the student. Within them are the various stages of the learning process, from the development of an initial learning question right through to the completed piece of work. They are a record of the challenges students have faced and how they have overcome them. They are a useful tool to track progress and can be used to engage students with the learning process, helping them to reflect not only on the subject content but also on how they learned it. I have used these with all year groups, from 7 to sixth form, and they serve as a valuable revision resource.

### Information technology

Even as I write this, I am fully aware that any advice or ideas I offer about the use of information technology may be soon be out of date. Therefore, I will suggest a number of methods of presentation that appear to have stood the test of time and a few more current ideas.

- Movies: These can be an excellent hook for a number of learners because they offer a visual representation of their learning question, combining images with text to explain processes, ideas or theories. They are also great for teachers to use as a learning aid at another time. The advantages are that movies tend to be highly motivational for many students because they are a blend of images, text and music/commentary. They are also a great medium for students to work with, offering challenge and engagement. The disadvantages are, however, that they do require a certain amount of expertise and know-how; thus, if you are not capable, you are reliant upon the students' knowledge (not that this is a bad thing, only that you may struggle to support or challenge students). Another disadvantage is that students tend to get caught up selecting relevant images or video clips and their knowledge and understanding, including the text, suffers as a result. Therefore, video creation may require more direct supervision or intervention.

- Podcasts: These are easy to create, requiring little specialist equipment. All you need is a microphone or camera that can capture audio files. It is necessary for the students to start by choosing a format for the podcast: Will it be just them talking? Will it be a conversation between two students or a debate? Having decided on the format, students need to focus on their topics or themes to produce a script of cue cards to speak from. It they are fluent and experienced with public speaking, then they may not need this support, but it is a useful aid to start with. Then it is just the case of capturing the audio; it can be as easy as that. If the students want to develop this further, there is free editing software available on the internet, and they can even upload the files onto social media to share with classmates.

- PowerPoint: This is probably the medium of choice for many students, simply because most students are confident in using it. Its advantages are that it is easy to use and can offer good ways to display information. Disadvantages are that it may not challenge the students or get them to push their boundaries and work outside of their comfort zones.

- Prezi: This is a more slick and sophisticated presentation tool. It may require some modelling or teaching, but students can quickly learn how to exploit its many useful features. Advantages are that it offers newer twists for presentations and it is easy to use. Disadvantages are that students can get too involved in the various animations and styles rather than understanding, selecting and clearly conveying their information.

- Powtoon: This is a free web tool for creating animated video presentations. Students can access the webpage, and there are a number of useful online tutorials to teach the students how it works and what to do. In a very short space of time, the students master the software and go on to produce some fantastic presentations, allowing them to develop their creativity along with subject knowledge.

## Templates

Templates, graphic organisers, support sheets – whatever you refer to them as – they are a presentational strategy that supports students in organising their work into a logical sequence or order. Thus, these can be very useful for groups of students who have difficulty organising their thinking or information gathered. The main advantage of templates is that they offer a scaffold for students to follow; students know when they have completed a section and they are clear about what comes next. The disadvantage is that templates can limit students' thinking. If students believe that all they have to do is complete the boxes, it

| The 5 Ws | To sum up |
|---|---|
| Who:<br><br>What:<br><br>When:<br><br>Where:<br><br>Why: | Summarise the text into six key points:<br>1)<br>2)<br>3)<br>4)<br>5)<br>6)<br>20 word summary: |

| Test it out | Part of the process |
|---|---|
| Research/learning question:<br><br>Method of data collection:<br><br>Results:<br><br>Conclusion: | Stage 1<br>Stage 2<br>Stage 3<br>Stage 4<br>Stage 5 |

**Figure 9.2** Example of four templates that could be used to support students

can stop them from challenging themselves to go above and beyond. It can stifle creativity. If we are telling them to just complete each section, where is the challenge in that?

## Stage 6: Review/reflect

This is the most important stage. It requires students to internalise what they have been learning about. Do they now know and understand the topic that they have been learning, or is knowledge still superficial, with a jazzy PowerPoint but no real grasp of the basic concepts? If all the stages have been completed to a satisfactory level, then success should be guaranteed and your aim for them to become independent learners, searching and solving, discovering and mastering has been achieved. Having completed their work, ask students to answer the questions on the guide sheet that supports this chapter. This should provide them with the stimuli to demonstrate their mastery and contemplate their learning journey. Allowing sufficient time for students to review their work and reflect on how they learned it is vital. It is, in fact, the most important stage.

## Stage 7: Test/assess/feedback

Once the project or investigation has been fully completed by students, now is the time to test their understanding, assess their work against the success criteria and offer constructive feedback on what went well and what they can do to improve.

### Test

This can be delivered in a number of ways: a question-and-answer session, a quick-fire quiz or a written test or exam. Whatever approach you take, bear in mind that when the students have been producing their own independent study, your test needs to be universal. It may be the case that you produce the test or exam prior to their investigation so you have some parameters for the students to work within.

### Assess

Using the success criteria will allow you to assess the work within clear guidelines. The marking is then transparent for both student and teacher. 'You scored . . . because you didn't include X, Y and Z as shown in the criteria'. There can be no complaints if you have referred to the criteria throughout the study and students helped to design them.

### Feedback

This is directly linked to the success criteria. The criteria set the benchmark for each level or expectation; therefore, in your feedback, you can quote directly from the rubric. Remember to praise the progress and focus on and be explicit about what was good about students' work. For more detail, refer to the chapter on feedback.

## When it goes wrong: Problem solving

If this is to be a truly challenging endeavour for the students, then it stands to reason that they will encounter problems and dips in motivation, as we all do. As 21st-century learners and as growing individuals, it is obvious that they will encounter challenges at times. The secret is how we cope with those setbacks.

Peer support can be a great tool to help students solve the problems. Sharing good practice during a review session or pairing up students for a short time may be all that is required for students to get each other back on track. Using your lead learner (as previously mentioned in the differentiation section) may go some way toward solving any issues. However, the best way to mitigate against problems is to provide students with ongoing feedback about their progress that they can easily understand and act upon. This progress feedback should concentrate on what they need to do to improve their work and offer steps on how to achieve this. Regular feedback serves two purposes: The first is to improve the academic achievement of the student and the second is to promote student motivation.

## Motivation

In a crude definition, motivation can be divided into two kinds: intrinsic and extrinsic. Intrinsic motivation describes internal motivation: that drive within you that makes you want to try new things or learn more about a topic to gain a deeper understanding. Independent learning is reliant upon intrinsic motivation, the students' desire to discover new knowledge and learn more about a given topic.

Extrinsic motivation is linked to external rewards or outcomes. For example, 'if you complete this work you can have a sweet' or 'the best piece of work wins a prize'. These motivational cues can work wonders with specific groups of children, but it can undermine the longer term intrinsic motivation we are trying to foster. That said, I believe that there is a time and a place for both, and it may be that when motivation is subsiding, the reward of a chocolate bar at the end of the lesson is all that is needed to kick-start a student.

The main point to remember is that motivation for an independent challenge should be higher than for other tasks because the students have taken ownership and assumed control of their own learning, established their own learning goals, and are finding the motivation from within to progress towards success. However, as problems arise, motivation can drop and ebb. The challenge is to find what can then be done to enthuse and inspire the students again. As mentioned above, feedback can be a major tool in achieving this.

Setting smaller, short term goals within the lesson can also help to make the larger task more manageable. Take students back to the planning stage: If this has been completed in detail, then students may just need a reminder of what step they are on and a positive word on how well they have done so far. If planning was not completed to your satisfaction, then now is the time to address the problem and revisit the steps necessary for success: Use the prompt questions to get the student back on track and reengaged with the challenge.

The key to motivation for 21st-century learners comes down to three principles:

- AUTONOMY: The freedom to self-govern is a huge motivator for many students; it is far easier to engage with students who are walking their own path rather than being dragged kicking and screaming down yours.

- MASTERY: Students are working towards mastering a specific area of the subject or topic they want to learn about. When students achieve mastery, their self-esteem rockets, giving them confidence that they can achieve in the subject, and an understanding that if they persevere and show grit they can be successful. This then acts as motivation for other challenges, creating a sense of self-worth and confidence that they have been successful before and they can be again. It's motivational because they want to repeat the emotions of achievement and fulfilment.

- PURPOSE: Having a sense of purpose is vital to achievement. Students need to know and believe that there is a point to them working so hard. Whether it is to achieve in their examinations or to win a prize, they have to have a sense of purpose. Related to purpose is the ability to postpone instant gratification. In his book, *The Un-heavenly City* (1970), Dr Edward Banfield aimed to discover what made some people more successful than others. He discovered two major characteristics of successful people: the ability to have a long term perspective and the ability to delay gratification. He recognised that people who want instant fulfilment, fun, enjoyment and an easy life have a lower economic status compared to those who are disciplined and endeavour to work hard; the latter achieve a higher economic status, improved self-esteem and personal satisfaction. In short, they have a higher purpose for their work: They recognise that working hard now will bring rewards in the future.

The point is that students now have three key motivators, both intrinsic and extrinsic, that drive, inspire and enthuse them to complete the challenge and therefore taste the success that both they and you want them to achieve. Remember, this should be challenging and, therefore, it will probably not run smoothly. In fact, if you truly want to create 21st-century learners and really immerse your students in study, it will often follow the following process:

# Messy to begin with – frustrating in the middle – and glorious at the end.

## Moving away from modelling, in a nutshell

- Assume the coaching role, take a step back and let students lead their own learning.

- Set realistic and specific learning questions.

- Develop success criteria that match the learning.

- Break projects down into smaller steps.

- Refer to these steps constantly.

- Support students' efforts in research when necessary; students can quickly go off track and fail to recognise bias.

- Make sure it is always their own work, set the standards high and expect the best.

- Give them choice when presenting.

- Review the process – not only what they learned but how they learned it.

- Offer feedback throughout.

- Motivate by remembering the three key principles of AUTONOMY, MASTERY and PURPOSE.

**Figure 9.3** Moving away from modelling, in a nutshell

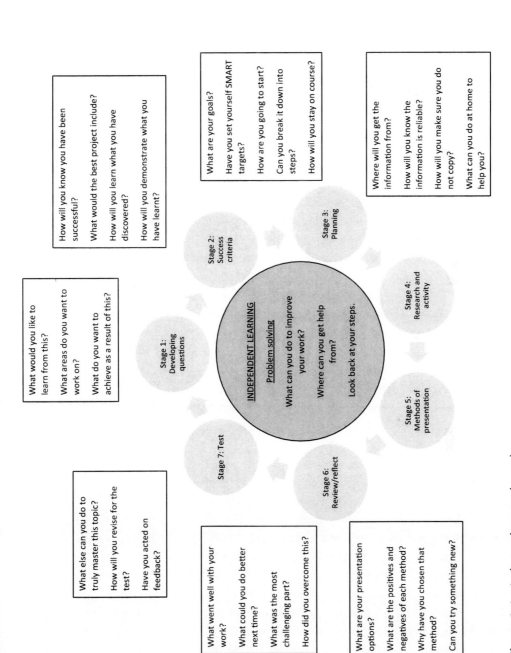

How will you know you have been successful?

What would the best project include?

How will you learn what you have discovered?

How will you demonstrate what you have learnt?

What are your goals?

Have you set yourself SMART targets?

How are you going to start?

Can you break it down into steps?

How will you stay on course?

Where will you get the information from?

How will you know the information is reliable?

How will you make sure you do not copy?

What can you do at home to help you?

What would you like to learn from this?

What areas do you want to work on?

What do you want to achieve as a result of this?

Stage 2: Success criteria

Stage 3: Planning

Stage 1: Developing questions

Stage 4: Research and activity

INDEPENDENT LEARNING

Problem solving

What can you do to improve your work?

Where can you get help from?

Look back at your steps.

Stage 7: Test

Stage 5: Methods of presentation

Stage 6: Review/reflect

What else can you do to truly master this topic?

How will you revise for the test?

Have you acted on feedback?

What went well with your work?

What could you do better next time?

What was the most challenging part?

How did you overcome this?

What are your presentation options?

What are the positives and negatives of each method?

Why have you chosen that method?

Can you try something new?

**Figure 9.4** Independent study cycle

# 10

# Literacy for learning

Good written and oral communication is vital to becoming a successful student and a successful citizen in later life. Not being able to express yourself, whether in conversation or in writing, is the single largest barrier to success. Therefore, you should embrace the task of teaching communication rather than shy away from it.

Whilst teaching at my first school as a young teacher who thought he had all the answers, I remember attending an afterschool training session on literacy. Much to my embarrassment now, I recall thinking, 'Literacy? What's this got to do with me? Just because the English department are no good, we have to pick up the pieces and do their job.' How naïve I was! I hasten to add that one of my current roles within school is Literacy Coordinator, so my penitence is done!

It's not actually about literacy. It's about outstanding teaching. Geoff Barton (2012) has a great way of looking at it: "If I am a teacher of history, I have to take responsibility to teach my students how to read and write and speak like a historian. That's not about literacy: It's about good teaching."

The reality is that each subject has its own nuances for communication. Science, for example, has a formal writing style: 'We added potassium to the test tube and heated the liquid for twenty seconds in the Bunsen burner. We recorded the reaction.'

English may approach the same experiment as follows: 'Alice clasped the test tube in one hand and tentatively added the silvery potassium. As the roaring flames danced around the tube, boom! A mighty explosion occurred.'

Both approaches are perfectly good, but they use very different writing styles. What's important is recognising this and sharing it with the students, teaching them how to read, write and talk like a historian, geographer, mathematician or scientist. Within departments, we each have our own way of talking about our subject. We have developed our own language conventions and vocabulary. It's the process of sharing this with students and teaching them the necessary literacy skills that is so important to ensure that they are successful in your subject. And if we spend a little more time each lesson developing those communication skills, the sum of all the parts could have a considerable effect on an individual's life possibilities.

Literacy can be divided into three parts: speaking, reading and writing. Below are a number of ideas to enhance your teaching of communication within your subject area.

## Speaking: You set the standards

You set the standards, so have high expectations. If you willingly accept one word answers, then that becomes the norm. It is habit forming, so when it comes to examinations and you find that the students are struggling to string a sentence together – well, sorry to be blunt, but that is a result of the speaking culture you have created in the classroom. There is a strong correlation between a student's verbal ability and his/her writing ability. If he/she is struggling to speak in a sentence, then there will undoubtedly be a struggle to write a sentence. However, it is not purely about translating what students say to their paper. It is more about developing a culture of learning dialogue within your classroom. Students are able to discuss with both the teacher and their peers what they are learning and how they are learning. That culture of talk can be created so all students have the confidence to speak, ask questions and formulate answers. All students contribute so you are not hearing from the same voices lesson after lesson.

The following ideas should help to encourage speaking and engagement within lessons.

1) **Speak in sentences:** Insist that students answer in full sentences. This one rule alone has had a considerable impact on the performance of my students. To begin with, this can seem laborious and time consuming – constantly having to remind them to put their answer in a sentence – but they soon pick up the practice. You may need to model the kind of language you are expecting or ask other students to support. For example, 'Susan, can you add to David's answer?' 'David, can you put that key term in a different sentence?' Bouncing the question can help to develop an understanding of what is expected.

2) **Wait time:** We all know this, but it is so difficult to do. Become more disciplined, give the students time to think, and not only think of the answer but think of an acceptable way to express it. It is one thing to know the answer is 1666; it's a different thing to be able to answer, 'The great fire of London began in Pudding Lane in 1066'. I know it can create that awkward silence, and you may be dying to jump in and help, but fight the urge. Stay disciplined and wait. The answers will come, I promise.

3) **Speaking activities:** Introduce more speaking activities into your lesson. Refer back to the starter activities, 'Rather be . . .' or 'What if . . .', which are two great ways to get students talking to each other and you. At my school, I introduced S.A.L.A.D. (Speaking And Listening Activity Day), which is a whole day spent without a pen. The concept is that the lesson involves a speaking activity or a range of speaking activities to promote communication skills. It was real challenge to start with, but both

staff and students embraced it, and we have seen a definite development in student participation within lessons and the improvement in spoken words has translated to improvements in the standard of written work.

4) **Make key words explicit:** Whenever you or your students say a key word, make reference to it. Whenever I hear a key term, I draw attention to it by telling the class, (for example, 'nice use of key words') and then I write it on the board. Part of my board is sectioned off just for this purpose, so as the lesson progresses I can add to the list. This then supports the students with their work as they can see the words on the board and they serve as a reminder to include the words in their work.

5) **Questioning:** This is covered in Chapter 7. But if you want KILLER answers, first make the questions high order questions from Bloom's Taxonomy. Ditch "what" and "when" and go for "how" and "why". Make sure you get Key terms, Impressive vocabulary, Linked ideas, Language is appropriate, English is formal and students Reflect.

6) **Talk templates:** I developed these for my school's PE department to use within lessons. Talk templates can be handed out so that when you are asking questions, students can refer to them to support their interaction. Then, as the students rehearse success and become more confident, the cards can be taken away and the standard of response will hopefully remain intact and the same. Figure 10.1 provides examples of four cards that can be adapted and developed for any subject.

7) **Give me an answer with the word . . . in it**: This is a great way to get students to structure answers and improve their impressive vocabulary. The teacher provides a

**Talk Templates 1**
I was impressed with . . .
Impressive Vocabulary:
• fluidity, elegance, complex, positive

**Talk Template 2**
Regarding . . .
Impressive Vocabulary:
• admirable, accomplished, graceful, sophisticated

**Talk Template 3**
On the other hand . . .
Impressive Vocabulary:
• powerful, spirited, restrained, promising

**Talk Template 4**
In summary . . .
Impressive Vocabulary:
• plethora, sensational, elaborate, mesmeric

**Figure 10.1**  Talk templates

key word or component of the answer and students structure an answer around it. Below are a few examples:

a.   Science:   'Give me an answer with the word **temperature** in it.'

'The metal expanded when there was an increase in **temperature**.'

b.   History:   'Give me an answer containing the word **plethora** in it.'

'The native Americans had a **plethora** of uses for the buffalo.'

8)   **Structuring formal talk 1:** Depending upon your region, county or even country, you may have a local dialect. Within the UK, we have a multitude of dialects and sub dialects within regions, each with their own particular conventions and styles. Add into this slang and we have a melting pot of lexicon. The issue is, like it or not, we need to teach our students how to speak and write using Standard English. If we want them to be successful at interviews and in the workplace, formal language is necessary. Therefore, we should correct informal language and slang. I understand how this may be uncomfortable, and I'm not saying regional language or colloquialisms should be lost. In fact, I love them, but recognising when and where we should use them is essential. For example, the word 'like' has percolated into my students' everyday language and it tends to precede many answers:

'What is the capital of Spain?'

'Erm like, Madrid'

'Like Madrid or just Madrid?'

As teachers we need to model formal talk and expect our students to converse in the same fashion. Keep standards high; model formal talk and correct slang.

9)   **Structuring formal talk 2:** To help establish formal talk and the use of Standard English within lessons, use a literacy mat or prompt card to remind and support students of vocabulary they should be using. The example in Table 10.1 can help students to increase and improve their vocabulary and over time this support can be withdrawn. Often when I teach a lesson that involves speaking activities such as a debate, I ask students to create their own prompt cards for homework; the results are always impressive. Following on from this, they can then create a number of prompts for a range of speaking activities, including persuasive speeches, monologues, presentations or storytelling.

10)   **No passengers:** As discussed in the questioning chapter, if you want students to talk more, you have to give them the opportunity to do so. Don't bother waiting for their hands to go up – you decide who you want to talk to. The steps and prompts from the 'no passengers' section in Chapter 7 will greatly increase participation from your class. It always saddens me to think that some of our students may go through the

**Table 10.1** Structuring formal talk

| To introduce an idea | To illustrate a point | To add a point | To sequence ideas | Conclusions | Impressive vocabulary |
|---|---|---|---|---|---|
| · Regarding | · As the research shows | · It must also be considered | · More importantly | · In conclusion | · Plethora |
| · In my opinion | · For example | · Firstly . . . secondly | · Not only that but | · To sum up | · Zenith |
| · The evidence suggests | · To demonstrate | · In addition to | · Subsequently | · To summarise | · Circumspect |
| · Firstly we must consider | · As evidence shows | · Furthermore | · Initially | · We can ascertain | · Cumulative |
| · Having considered | · The results indicate | · Consequently | · Following on from | · Overall | · Appease |
| | | | | | · Superfluous |
| | | | | | · Complacent |

whole of the day and not have one conversation or word with a teacher. Resolve to attempt to speak to every student in your class every lesson. I know it may not be realistic, but make it an aim so that at least you speak to far more than you used to.

## Reading: How to get students to engage with text and read with purpose

Reading is key for knowledge acquisition, yet it feels at times that reading has become considered geeky or unfashionable and has lost its relevance in the classroom. If we, as teachers, don't hold it in high regard or accentuate its importance, then the students certainly won't. For me, reading is the gateway to learning. How else can you know the thoughts of the Dalai Lama or the contemplations of Winston Churchill? All the greatest ideas, theories and people have had something written about them or, in the latter case, written something themselves. It is from reading and learning that we can grow as people. Below are ten techniques to use to inspire a passion for reading within your classroom.

1) **Reciprocal reading:** This is a practice widely used at primary schools, and having seen it used, I wonder why it is not more commonly integrated within the secondary classroom. It involves students actively engaging with text to improve their understanding and comprehension of both fiction and nonfiction. It involves four challenges for students to consider:

   **Challenge 1 – Predict:** Having given the book, page numbers or text to the students, the teacher challenges them to predict what they will be reading about and what will happen. If there are any, they can use visual cues from the pages to help them as they attempt to predict what the text will include and discuss. This can be recorded in their book or just discussed as a class. They can use the following sentence stems:

   I think this text is about . . .

   I predict . . .

   I think I will learn about . . .

   I imagine . . .

   Students then read the text to discover if they are correct in their predictions. They can record the differences before and after, if you wish. This activity may necessitate a certain amount of guidance from the teacher. For example, if the title of the chapter is 'The Great Fire of London', then students may respond to the question by simply stating, 'I think this text is about the great fire of London'. This is when intervention is necessary to push students further and ask, 'And what do you think you will learn about the great fire of

London?' That question is needed to push them to consider more deeply what the text may include.

**Challenge 2 – Question:** As students read the text, you may ask them to engage with some or all of the following lower level question stems. Again, this involves students becoming active with the text rather than passively skim reading and not absorbing the information or making connections.

Who . . .?

What . . .?

When . . .?

Where . . .?

Why . . .?

How . . .?

Which . . .?

What if . . .?

How ought . . .?

Describe . . .

**Challenge 3 – Clarify:** This challenge tests the comprehension skills of the students: Have they really understood what they have just read? You may need to prompt students to reread the text or try to connect to other concepts or ideas that they have been learning about. This is also an opportunity for students to record questions to clarify. As students read the text, they may have questions that they want to ask to clarify their understanding of the topic, or they may be curious about a certain point. For example, 'Where exactly was Pudding Lane in London, where the great fire started?' These questions can be noted in their exercise books or recorded on sticky notes that the students can then put on the board to engage with later. You can ask the students to come to the board and select three questions that they then have to go away to research and answer, either in the lesson or as homework for the next lesson. Possible question stems for students are below. Ask them to write down any questions that they may have about the text.

I didn't get . . .

What does . . . mean?

I don't understand . . .

Can you explain . . .

Challenge 4 – **Summarise:** This challenge requires higher level thinking from students. They are asked to summarise and prioritise the text they have just read, dissecting the text and picking out the most important points. Then they can be asked to prioritise those points. As the teacher, you may want to confine this activity to six key points from the text and then number them in order of priority. One subsidiary challenge may be to reduce the six key points to six key words (and then perhaps to one key word to sum up the whole text).

To read more about reciprocal teaching at work, see Lori D. Oczkus' (2010) *Reciprocal Teaching at Work: Powerful Strategies and Lessons for Improving Reading Comprehension.*

2) **Storyboards:** This activity has been around for many years, but it is a wonderful activity to get students to select key points and visually represent the text. It also serves as a great way to revise. Students select the most relevant points and, depending upon what you require, they may write a caption underneath or you may ask them to represent the text with pictures but without any words. Students can be then be challenged to retell the story using the pictures as cues. This can be used in many situations, to represent a recipe in Food Technology, the life of Christ in RE, a fitness programme in PE, the production process in Design and Technology or the Industrial Revolution in History.

3) **Just a minute:** Having read a text, students are challenged to talk about that subject matter for a minute without repetition, hesitation or deviation from the topic. This can be carried out in pair or groups. If student X is unable to complete the challenge, then student Y takes over on the same subject until the one minute is up. You may give each group different texts and have individuals move around the groups, sharing their information.

4) **Reading questions:** Students may struggle to interpret questions, especially exam style questions. Annotating the question or rewriting the question can help to improve students' understanding. Give the definitions of command words, such as *describe* and *explain*, to ensure students know the difference between the two. Ask students to give alternative words for key terms in the question, thus making sure all students understand all aspects of the question before they attempt to answer it.

5) **What went wrong?** This challenge involves a pre-prepared piece of text with a number of literacy and/or subject-specific mistakes within it. This could be something the teacher has written, a copy of a previous student's work or an anonymous piece of student work from another class or group. I would advise against using a student's work in front of him/her as it can be demoralising to critique work in front of the peer group, even anonymously. The challenge for the students is to then unpick the text and discover how many mistakes they can spot.

An example from a history lesson.

> when the normans first invaded britian in 1088 their was alot of destruction and fighting. The battle of hastings was when the normans took power William of Normandy was claiming the English throne and he had to defet Harold goodwinson Harold was killed on the battle field by an arrow fired from one of the French archers that struck him in the eye. William was then crowned king on Christmas day.

> when the normans first invaded britian in 1088 their was alot of destruction and fighting. The battle of hastings was when the normans took power William of Normandy was claiming the English throne and he had to defet Harold goodwinson Harold was killed on the battle field by an arrow fired from one of the French archers that struck him in the eye. William was then crowned king on Christmas day.

Having gone through correcting errors in the text with the students, your next challenge can be for them to improve the paragraph. What else could they include? How could they improve the structure of the written work? They could have a go at writing their own paragraph containing mistakes for a partner to analyse. This activity could be used to self or peer assess any piece of extended writing that the students produce. Turning the activity into more of a game motivates the students to engage more with the text, so instead of, 'Read through your work and check for mistakes', this becomes 'Swap books and play what went wrong' or 'Try to spot as many mistakes as you can in your work or your partner's work'. They enjoy the challenge and students are sometimes more inclined to accept a critique from the comfort of an informal one-to-one discussion with another student.

6)  **Reading Races:** Skimming and scanning are two widely known approaches to speed reading texts: They allow you to read though a vast amount of text quickly and can be efficient and effective techniques to aid study.

    Skimming: When you skim read, your eyes dart across the page, trying to ascertain the gist or overall ideas of the text. To help students to skim read, teach them the three steps to effective skimming:

    a)  Read the entire first paragraph. This often gives you the structure to the text to follow. For example, in a Geography text it might introduce the cause, effect and response to an earthquake. Students can therefore predict that if they want to learn about how people responded to the earthquake, the information will be nearer the bottom of the text.

    b)  Read the first sentence of each new paragraph. In most cases, this will give you the main ideas of the paragraph.

c) Read the final paragraph completely because this often serves as a summary to all that has been discussed in the text.

Scanning: This is the fastest method of speed reading, but does not require that you understand anything within the text. It is very useful if you are trying to find specific details – for example names, dates or places. Again, there are three simple principles to follow:

a) Concentrate on the word, fact or detail you are searching for: It is likely to appear more clearly in the text.

b) Look for the words in bold or italics as these can help you as you search through the text.

c) Use your finger to run across the page under the line of writing. However, let your finger run slightly faster than your eyes. You will find that this drags your eyes across the page quicker.

Once you have defined these two approaches to speed reading, these techniques can be used in 'Reading Races'. You can divide your class into groups and give them all the same text. At your desk, you'll have a series of questions to give to each group of students. On the instruction, 'On your marks, get set, go', students race to your desk to collect the first question related to the text. Once they have found the answer by employing the skimming and scanning techniques, they then write it down and race back to the teacher to check if the answer is correct. You can then send them back to find the correct answer, to improve their answer or to find the answer to the next question. I normally produce ten questions to keep students engaged throughout as they can soon become disheartened if they fall well behind the rest of the class. I also produce a mixture of long and short response questions – consider how long you want them sitting at their desks searching for answers. The element of competition always creates a vibrant classroom with students desperately searching through text to find the answers. It's rare to find them so transfixed with text.

This is a fantastic technique to captivate a class. However, it is important to realise that it is unlikely to support their deeper understanding or knowledge of a topic. It serves as a great way to engage a class, but the students may not necessarily understand what they are writing down. You will probably need to go over the key points again. I often do a repeat test of the questions as a plenary to see what they can recall or to discover if they have lost the information already.

7) **Twenty words a minute:** Having read a piece of text, students are challenged to write down twenty words associated with it within a minute. The students have to think rapidly to complete the task and, in my experience, they find this challenge both frustrating, if their list is incomplete, and rewarding, if they meet the deadline.

8) **Live reading:** This requires the teacher to read to the class. As the teacher reads, students jot down thoughts, ideas or emotions from the text. You may want to stop at the end of each paragraph to ask the students to note something down for each paragraph. Thus, rather than the students sitting passively, they are engaged and listening carefully to the teacher. I make this challenge very open, allowing them to draw, produce a timeline, or draw emojis to tell the story of the text.

9) **Reading aloud:** Try to take every opportunity to encourage student participation within your lesson. Ask the students to read from the textbook or presentation rather than doing it yourself. I realise that some students may be reticent to reading since they often feel embarrassed or shy to read in front of others. However, if you can create a culture of reading aloud every lesson, whether this is their own work from their book, from the textbook or even as part of the starter activity, it will develop confidence and the acceptance of reading.

For those students who are particularly determined not to read, it is important not to ignore them. I engage them by asking them to read the first three sentences. Then, once they have finished, I may say "Well read – carry on" or "Fab, finish the paragraph, thank you". In most cases, having started reading they will comply with my instruction, so each time I'm extending the amount they are reading. Also, stopping them after three sentences allows me to choose somebody else if they have made several mistakes, and I can see that they are not comfortable enough to carry on.

10) **Text mystery:** This technique has been around for a while, but it is great to engage the students with close reading. Take a piece of text and mix it up. The challenge is then for the students to piece it back together in an order. It stretches students, making them consider chronology of events, how text fits together, and sequencing. They have to close read to understand and order the text, thus engaging with it at a higher level than if it was just a normal page of text.

11) **Reading groups:** This involves groups of students reading in silence. What could be better? Groups are given the same text to read in silence. Having read, they then discuss what they have read and develop three questions based upon the text. There is an opportunity for you to give different groups different texts, and then group envoys move around the class to discuss the different texts and report back to their group.

12) **Speed reading:** There are a number of apps or software that will enable you to put a piece of text through a speed reading device. You are able to set the speed of the number of words per minute and size of the text. It allows your students to access large amounts of text rapidly, as well as being a fun and novel way to read. Subsequent challenges may involve writing a brief summary of what they have just read or jotting down ten key words they read in the text.

# Writing: How to get quality written work

Writing is a fundamental aspect to education. It is how we present ideas and thoughts, how we demonstrate what we know and understand and how we display our talents. Of course, not every subject has a written assessment, but writing is the device by which students are examined and consequently graded/scored against. Therefore, if students are going to be successful, they must develop the ability to write with clarity and purpose.

Getting students to write with extension, clarity and purpose can be a challenge for any teacher. The first thing to consider is when you will present the opportunities for students to write within your lessons. Do you ask them to write down their starter activity? Do they answer questions in full sentences? Do they have to write longer response answers or essays? Having considered when they write within your lesson, consider next what guidance you give them with each of the above questions. Students won't just write outstanding 2000-word essays or instinctively consider the audience of their prose. They need to be taught how to craft written work, and that's our job. Many times I have observed a lesson in which the teacher is berating students for shoddy work because they have not written in full sentences or their answers lack detail, and I think to myself, "Well, you didn't ask them to". Now I know that students should understand the protocols and conventions of written work, but unless you have developed those skills so that they become a habit for the students, you will often be faced with work that has not met your expectations. So the challenge is to develop writing habits that can be employed by the student time and time again, and that can be transferred from subject to subject across the curriculum.

# Developing writing habits

1.  **Structure:** For an outstanding piece of extended writing, there needs to be a degree of structure. This involves writing in paragraphs, with an engaging introduction and a concise conclusion. You can support your students by helping them to develop the content for each paragraph. You may need to remind them of the TIPTOP rule (i.e., you move on to a new paragraph when you change Time, Place, Topic or Person). This reminder of structure may be all your class needs to then progress with the challenge, or you may need to give additional support to your students. This is where differentiation will be applied. For those requiring additional support, ask what they think needs to go into each paragraph to help them to structure their work before they start. You can provide sentence stems to start them thinking or even model an answer. A powerful technique is to type or write the opening to an answer in front of the students, with their guidance. I ask them, 'How could we start this answer off?' Then we craft an answer together. This can be a messy process, with me deleting and rewriting new ideas from students, but that is the point. I model that messy process. Remember the idea: Messy to begin with – frustrating in the middle – and glorious at the end.

# Literacy mat

## Tips for great writing:

- Every sentence starts with a capital letter. Use a capital letter for names and places.
- Every sentence finishes with a punctuation mark. Either: ? ! or.
- Remember the TIPTOP rule. Start a new paragraph whenever you change time, place, topic or person.
- Vary the length of your sentences. Short sentences at the start and end of paragraphs can add clarity.
- Include impressive vocabulary to engage the reader.

## Making links

Because...

Therefore...

As a result of...

Due to...

Consequently...

This means that...

## Making points

To begin with...

Furthermore...

In addition...

Firstly, secondly, finally.

What is more...

## Making comparisons

As with...

Likewise...

Equally...

Similarly...

Correlate...

Compared with...

## Giving examples

For example...

As shown by...

Such as...

...demonstrates...

For instance...

As proven by...

## Emphasising points

Above all...

More importantly...

Especially...

Mainly...

In particular...

Most often...

## Transition words

either...

besides...

whilst...

hence...

initially...

regardless...

## Making contrasts

Alternatively...

Whereas...

Despite this...

Although...

However...

Nevertheless...

## Conclusions

In conclusion...

To summarise...

Overall...

To conclude...

In brief...

On the whole...

REFLECT: Proof read your work

Does every sentence begin with a capital letter and end with a punctuation mark?

Have I checked my spellings?

## Common command words

| | | |
|---|---|---|
| **Describe** - Give the main characteristics of something. "What does it look like?" | **Account for** - Give an explanation / reasons for. | **Compare** - Describe the similarities **and** differences of at least two things. |
| **Explain** - Give reasons **why** something happens. The points in the answer **must be linked.** | **Define** - Give the meaning of a word, phrase or concept. | **Evaluate** - Pick out good and bad points and make judgements. |
| **Outline** - Provide a brief account of relevant information/Summarise the main points of something. | **Discuss** - Set out both sides of an argument (for and against), and come to a conclusion. | **Annotate** - Add detail to a diagram or image. Add words that describe and/or explain the features. |

## Impressive Vocabulary

| | | | |
|---|---|---|---|
| **Big** | substantial, great, huge, sizeable, gigantic, extensive | **Estimate** | calculate, judge, determine, consider, evaluate |
| **Small** | compact, miniscule, diminutive, tiny | **Similar** | identical, corresponding, indistinguishable, alike |
| **Issue** | topic, subject, matter, problem | **Important** | noteworthy, significant, critical, major, crucial |
| **Factor** | part, element, component, feature, characteristic, item | **Many** | numerous, countless, plethora (too many), multiple |
| **Benefit** | advantage, reward, virtue, aid, bonus, merit | **Problem** | difficulty, drawback, obstacle, complication, dilemma |

### Writing Style

Purpose: What are you writing for? To explain? To persuade?

Intended audience: Who are you writing for?

Genre: What category of writing is it? A speech? A recipe?

Style: What is the writing style? Formal or informal?

### Have I written a KILLER answer?

K – Keywords

I – Impressive vocabulary

L – Linked ideas

L – Language (full sentences)

E – English as standard

R – Reflective (could I make it better?)

**Figure 10.2** Literacy mat

2. **Connectives and keywords:** As mentioned in the modelling chapter, when I ask my students to complete a piece of writing I will often provide them with a literacy mat. This has lists of key connectives to help students to link ideas and thus improve their work. Prior to them starting to write, we will, as a class, have created a list of key words that we think can be included in our answer to enhance the work and demonstrate our knowledge and understanding of the topic. I then challenge the students to use as many of the connectives and key words in their work as possible. I give out two different coloured highlighters, and the students develop their own key, one colour for connectives and one for key words. Then, as they proof read their work, they highlight all the connectives and key words that they have used. The student who uses the most wins a prize. I say prize, but this tends to entail having a small trophy on his/her desk or using the electric pencil sharpener!

3. **Literacy targets:** You may want to highlight the importance of certain literary devices by making specific targets for the students to work towards and achieve. This may be a generic class target or a personalised target for the students to note down in their books when you are marking. Figure 10.4 shows some of the targets I use within my lessons.

**Table 10.2** Literacy targets

| Literacy target | Target | How to achieve your target |
|---|---|---|
| LT1 | Structure your work by writing in paragraphs. | Remember the TIPTOP rule. Start a new paragraph when you change Time, Place, Topic or Person. Plan out your answer first. |
| LT2 | Link ideas together by using connectives. | Use your connective mat to help you link ideas together and to develop the point you are trying to make. *So, because, although, despite, in addition.* |
| LT3 | Use impressive vocabulary throughout your work. | Use the thesaurus to come up with alternative words. |
| LT4 | Use key words in your writing. | Use the key words on the board or on the wall in your writing. |
| LT5 | Use full stops and capital letters consistently. | Remember, every sentence starts with a capital letter. Every sentence finishes with a .?! Proper nouns need a capital letter; these include people and places. |
| LT6 | Check your spellings. | Use the dictionary or word mats to check you are spelling correctly. Sound the word out in your head; this may help. |
| LT7 | Proof read your work. | Close read your work to check that it makes sense and to spot any errors. Read using a pencil under each word to really make sure you are checking. |
| LT8 | Read your questions carefully so you fully understand what you are being asked to do. | Highlight key words or command words. Use the dictionary and thesaurus to check that you understand the meanings of words or to look for similar words. |

| Literacy target | Target | How to achieve your target |
|---|---|---|
| LT9 | Use a range of sentences. | Use short sentences at the start of a paragraph. Use a mix of simple, compound and complex sentences. |
| LT10 | Check your punctuation. | Remember that every sentence must finish with a.?! Use apostrophes for possession or to replace a letter. The boy's football (possession) They're (replacement for they are) |

4.  **Modelling:** As previously mentioned in the chapter on modelling, if you want students to be successful, show them what success looks like. I have a number of display boards around my room showcasing good practice that I can pull off the wall and distribute around the class. Each board illustrates a good example of different styles of written work. I have a board for writing to explain, one for writing to persuade and another to show how to interpret graphs. These boards can save time and save me from having to repeat myself. I simply stick them up at the front of the class and tell students that if they are unsure or need to check that they are on track, they should come and look at the example board.

5.  **Sentence design:** To improve the literary ability of our students and to engage the reader, encourage students to use a range of different sentences – not only short and long but also simple, compound and complex. Referring to these sentence styles within your lesson will help students transfer their knowledge between subjects.

    Simple sentences: These contain a subject and a verb (for example: Susan likes to play football).

    Compound sentences: These join two simple sentences together (for example: Susan likes to play football, but she prefers rugby).

    Complex sentences: A complex sentence joins together one (or more) simple sentences with one (or more) clauses that cannot stand alone as a sentence (for example: Susan likes to play football, but she prefers rugby because it is more exciting).

6.  **Developing vocabulary:** This technique can be used when introducing specialist terms within your subject. I find it works best with the more technical words because the activity requires deeper thinking from the students. It can also be used as a homework activity to improve students' understanding of key terms. Students can complete the following template to develop their subject-specific vocabulary.

7.  **Writing conventions:** Within the classroom, students are asked to write for a number of different purposes. Making these explicit to students can go a long way toward achieving the outcome you desire. There are a number of styles that are commonly used in the classroom: writing to inform, explain, describe, persuade, to argue and for instruction. Each style has its own particular conventions, but discussing these with the

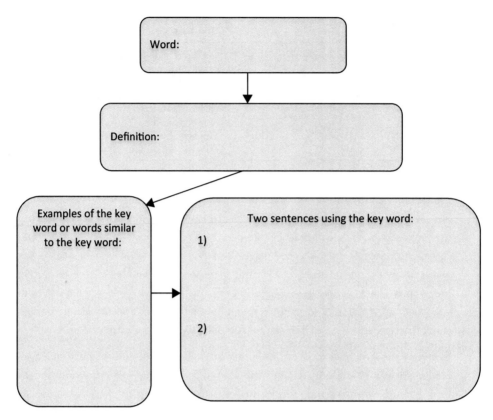

**Figure 10.3**   Developing vocabulary

students can help to clarify what you require and therefore how to progress towards that goal. Make the writing explicit by getting the students to consider the following:

Purpose – What are you writing for? (to explain, to persuade, to inform)

Intended audience – Who are you writing for? (a friend, the prime minister)

Genre – What category of writing is it? (a speech, a recipe, a science experiment)

Style – What is the style of writing? (formal or informal)

When you discuss PIGS with the students, they should recognise how they can transfer the skills they have learned in other subjects to yours. For example, if I want my students to write instructions to explain how they worked out a particularly difficult calculation, I could remind them that I want it written in the same style that you would use to write a recipe in a Food Technology lesson. Highlighting those transferable skills can help the students to achieve in your lesson.

8.  **Spelling:** Spelling is a significant feature of successful writing and communication. We can support our students by teaching them spelling strategies. These strategies can be divided into three approaches:

a) Sounds: How does the word sound? Sound it out with them. Each subject will have common words that are frequently misspelt, so one approach is to sound those words out with them. This can be linked to the next approach: visual cues. Write them on the board as you sound them out with exaggeration: *en-vi-ron-ment* instead of *enviroment*, *oct-a-he-dron* instead of *ocohedron*.

b) Visual: Show them what the word looks like. Break it down and sound it out: *tem-per-a-ture*.

c) Mnemonics: These can be very useful for commonly misspelt words:

Necessary: Never eat cakes eat salmon sandwiches and remain young

Because: Big elephants can always understand small elephants

I have several of the more common subject-specific words displayed around the classroom with a number of mnemonics to help remember how to spell them correctly.

9. **Writing talk:** Give students the opportunity to discuss what they are going to write. This could be a group activity or within pairs. The chance to orally rehearse what they are about to write allows the students thinking time so they can consider their work before putting pen to paper.

10. **Writing Time:** If you want outstanding written work, then you must give the students adequate time to produce it. Some students may be confident with the writing challenge and begin straight away, and others may want to carefully consider each paragraph and plan out their response. Both are perfectly acceptable approaches, but time must be given to allow students to complete the task to their satisfaction.

## Dialogue to support literacy

**Speaking:**

'Give me that answer in a sentence.'

'Think about it, I'm coming back to you.'

'Nice use of key terms, well done.'

'Can you give me an answer with some impressive vocab in it?'

'Give me an answer with the word . . . in it.'

'Can you give me that answer again using formal language . . . thank you.'

**Reading:**

'What do you think this text is going to be about?'

'Guess what is going to happen next?'

'What do you think we will be learning about today?'

'What equipment do you think we will need today, based on the title?'

'Susan, can you clarify what has happened so far in the text?'

'What does the word . . . mean?'

'Can you give me another word for . . .?'

'Do you have any curiosity questions based on what we have just read?'

**Writing:**

'What could we include in each paragraph?'

'Remember the TIPTOP rule.'

'The student who includes the most connectives wins a prize.'

'Use the display boards to see examples of great work.'

---

### Literacy for learning, in a nutshell

- If you want outstanding historians, scientists and artists, then you must teach them how to speak, read and write like outstanding historians, scientists and artists.

- Speaking: You set the standards within your classroom; don't accept one word answers and only accept formal language.

- Promote impressive vocabulary and the use of key words by highlighting their use within lessons.

- Reading: Develop active reading skills by asking the students to predict, question, clarify and summarise text.

- Ask students to read aloud rather than you doing so.

- Writing: Writing is a process that is often messy to begin with, frustrating in the middle and glorious at the end.

- Get students to plan and structure their written work before they start writing.

- Set literacy targets for the students.

- Use literacy mats to develop writing skills; these can be withdrawn as students develop good writing habits.

**Figure 10.4** Literacy for learning, in a nutshell

# 11

# Classroom management

I questioned whether to write this chapter at all. If we are outstanding teachers or aspiring outstanding teachers, then we have probably cracked classroom management, right? But then I thought back to all those difficult classes I have taught over the years, and I came to realise that it was learning to deal with those challenges that has helped me become an outstanding teacher. That sounds trite, and I don't mean it to be. I had to learn the hard way. When I started at my second school, within one month we were in special measures. I was a new teacher, it was tough, and I remember crying some nights, thinking, 'I don't know how I am going to deal with these classes tomorrow.' However, working hard, being resourceful and learning from colleagues, I turned it around, and I hope that applying the techniques and strategies in this chapter will help you improve your practice. These techniques will help even with classes that are not problematic, and now when I teach new classes, I go through the same routines to reinforce the rules and make my expectations clear to the students.

First let me explain why you need to be open minded to these techniques. We all work at different schools, within different communities, with different groups of students, but fundamentally kids are kids. You may not agree with this idea. In fact, I hear it all the time at meetings or conferences – staff muttering to one another, 'Oh, that's fine for him/her, but it wouldn't work at our school, not with our kids'. It's probably the same staff who then say, 'Well, what do you expect with that class? You can't do anything with 'um'. I'm sorry, but I don't accept that. I have worked in a number of settings, with children with behavioural difficulties, in rural schools and in urban schools, and I've yet to find a child who didn't have the same basic needs and wants. Therefore, regardless of your own particular circumstances, I believe that if you practise the following techniques you can dramatically improve your performance in the classroom.

## Planning

This is essential to successful classroom management. As the saying goes, proper preparation prevents poor performance. For me, it's all in the planning. It starts with an effective

95

seating plan. Speak to colleagues before you start teaching your classes to discover which students can be challenging or which students don't work well together. Then work out where you want them in your classroom. Remember, it's your classroom, so you decide who goes where, not the students. As a general rule, I put my most challenging student under my nose at the front, then I seat the rest of the class boy/girl, boy/girl alphabetically. Don't be afraid to mix it up throughout the year if you think it isn't working. A good seating plan can help to reduce a myriad of issues.

What are your barriers to learning? And what can you do to mitigate against them? These are two key questions I ask myself when I am planning a lesson. What if the DVD player doesn't work? What if they forget their homework? What if Susan plays up? I then consider what actions I need to take to minimise disruption so that the lesson can continue to flow. As an example, let us consider those three questions.

What if the DVD player doesn't work? I can use the textbooks that cover the same topic area and get the students to create a storyboard from the text.

What if they forget their homework? We need the research homework to use in the lesson. I will print off some copies of key text in case anyone forgets. Or I can use the homework from the other class and share the resources.

What if Susan plays up? I must remember to greet her at the door and remind her that I want a great lesson today. Then I will ensure she fully understands what she needs to do and go to her first to make sure she is engaging with the challenge.

This may appear simplistic, but thinking about what barriers you may face helps you to cope with them if they do occur. Then, with practice, you learn to adapt your response as you foresee and deal with issues before they happen.

## Routine

Having routines and procedures helps everyone to understand what is expected. Expect the best by having outstanding routines. From giving out worksheets to answering questions, set routines can help eliminate a number of barriers. Some of these ideas may seem old hat, yet I see staff failing to carry them out on a daily basis, and they wonder why they have problems.

**Meet and greet:** Greet your students at the door. This can help break down barriers from the outset with certain students. Try to be as positive as possible in your first interaction with each student: A friendly smile or a little joke is all that is needed to set the tone of your lesson. Remember, every day is new with no mistakes in it. Don't carry baggage from one lesson to the next. Greet the student who was hell last lesson with the same warmth as the 'golden' student. (If there was a problem last lesson, then it needs to be resolved prior to this lesson.) If necessary, try to give an instruction after a greeting, so instead of the first thing you say to a student being, 'Oi, tuck your shirt in', it becomes,

'Morning Susan, you were fab last lesson, same again today thank you, and can you tuck your shirt in, thank you'.

**Starters:** As mentioned in the starter chapter, having an activity on the board for the students to do as soon as they come into the class gives you the time to sort out any issues with lack of equipment, uniforms etc. If this is routine, students will know that they have to come in and get on with the starter without you having to deliver a big introduction to the task.

**Books/worksheets/equipment:** When you can have these on the desks before the lesson begins, it makes the start of lesson slick. Thus you are able to command the class from the front so that you can see everyone, rather than behind students' backs giving them the opportunity to be off task or disruptive. I have a pocket full of pens and paper on my desk, and as I am talking I can be scanning the class looking for those students who I think need equipment. I can deal with equipment issues swiftly, giving out what is needed without disturbing the start of the lesson. You may have a school policy on equipment, and I have tried a number of strategies, but I have resolved that life is too short to worry about lending pens out. You may disagree; each to his own.

If you need to hand out resources during the lesson, try to minimise the time students are off task by considering when and how you will give the resources out. For example, you may have the opportunity to hand out worksheets whilst students are engaged with another activity, thus minimising disruption. Another approach is to give a selected student a time limit on how long they have to hand out resources or make it a competition of which row of students can give out the resources the fastest. Whatever strategy you use, the aim is to reduce the time students are off task and therefore reduce behavioural issues.

**Challenges/activities/questions:** Develop your own routines for these three components of a lesson. For me, I have a set procedure for introducing challenges and activities, which I discuss in the next section. I follow the guidelines for questioning as mentioned in Chapter 7.

**Effective instructions:** Whenever I introduce a challenge or activity, I go through the same routine. I first ensure that all students are listening. Then I break the challenge down into steps and I make sure that I don't overload them with too much information. If they need to know more, I can tell them the other stages once they have begun. Having given them the instructions, I then ask a student to repeat back to me what they have to do. I may then ask him/her to elaborate on the instruction. I will then ask another student the same thing. At this point, I may ask a student who struggles to retain information or a student who I don't think was listening properly. This prevents them from asking me later or being off task when the challenge begins. The quality of the instruction can help to minimise disruption. Staff who fail to give clear, effective instructions and then start activities are often faced with a barrage of questions and students off task and talking, for which they blame the students. It is the quality of the instructions that makes the difference.

## Example:

Compare these two instructions for the same task:

**Instruction 1:**

'Right, we've read through the text; now I want you to storyboard the information like we've done before. OK, off you go'.

**Instruction 2:**

'In a minute when I say go, I want you to read through the text on page 18 and storyboard eight key points – the eight points you consider to be the most important. Susan, what have you got to do?'

'Storyboard'

'Storyboard what, Susan?'

'The text'

'The text from where, Susan?'

'Page . . . I can't remember'

'Somebody remind her.'

'Page 18'

'Thank you. How many pictures are you going to do?'

'Eight'

'Brilliant. Thank you. Does anyone have any questions, queries or concerns? I will write up the key instructions on the board and the lead learner will come round and help you out if you are stuck. OK, go.'

This makes a huge difference to the flow of the lesson. Don't be lazy with instructions; poor instructions only create more work for you later as you run around the class spinning plates trying to deal with six or seven students who don't know what to do. Depending upon your class, a series of visual pictures can greatly help with instructions. The previous instruction may have visual cues such as a picture of a student reading a book with page 18 written next to it, then a picture of a storyboard with '8' written beside it. Two simple pictures to convey to the class what they need to do.

## Dealing with conflict

There are a few key rules to remember when dealing with conflict and disruptive students.

1.  **It's not necessarily about you:** As teachers, we aspire to have outstanding lessons every day with thirty beaming faces looking up at us and hanging off our every word. The reality can be very different. You may have planned the most exciting lesson, and yet it can still be disrupted by certain students' behaviour. It's worth remembering that their behaviour does not automatically stem from your interaction with the students; their poor behaviour could be linked to issues outside of the classroom. The students we teach come from a wide variety of backgrounds and situations, and we will never be able to fully empathise with their lives. Some students may have been up all night dealing with their crying baby brother, or trying to cope with an alcoholic parent – it's very difficult to ascertain why a student is behaving in a particular way, but sometimes it's out of our control and all we can do is manage the behaviour once it presents itself. Also, speak to colleagues and to find whether that same student displays poor behaviour in many classes and not just yours. Ask their advice and find out their coping strategies: What they do that is successful? Speak to your pastoral team or safeguarding representative if you have issues or concerns, and they may be able to give you guidance and put your mind at ease.

2.  **They are children and you are the adult:** It's often easy to get dragged into a childish argument with a student. Take a deep breath and remember that they are only twelve, thirteen or fourteen years old. Whatever their age, they are younger than you, they have not experienced the things you have, they have not lived a life outside of school, they have yet to mature physically and mentally and they are not the worldly wise citizens they consider themselves to be. Acknowledge the fact that you are the adult and act like the adult. Be professional. Screaming at a student in the corridor is never a good look.

3.  **You must follow through on warnings:** One of the biggest mistakes I witness when observing is staff not following through on warnings. It undermines you and your authority and tells students that you are inconsistent. The message that you send out becomes confusing. For example, 'Do that again and I will send you out'. Yet when the student does it again it is only to be met with, 'Last chance, don't do it'. Then, in the next lesson, you send the same student out after one warning about similar behaviour. The students know that you are inconsistent, and they can then argue that last lesson the behaviour was accepted. Inconsistency just creates problems. As a mentor once told me, if you say 'Do that again and I'll throw you out of the window', then if they do it again you have to throw them out the window! Keep your warnings realistic and follow through.

4.  **Treat them with respect, as adults, unless they behave otherwise:** It's important to treat everybody equally, fairly and with respect. I treat all students as adults until they behave otherwise. I say 'Good morning' when I greet them, I ask them politely to give out equipment if necessary, and I apologise if I need to. I believe this sets the tone and level of expectation within the class. If I ask politely to borrow a pencil, I expect the same level of politeness back. You set the standards within the classroom. A key

point, attributed to Andy Vass, is to always say 'thank you' and not 'please' when giving instructions. Because 'please' sounds as if you're begging, whereas 'thank you' presumes a positive response, and that the instruction will be followed straight away. A tip here is to then break eye contact or walk away, this action reinforces the expectation that the instruction will be followed through and stops a stand of situation from occurring. Give a little time for the student to respond in accordance with the instruction and, if they do not, then go back and with direct eye contact repeat the instruction, again followed by 'thank you'. In the majority of cases, this will suffice. So having set the tone, expect the best. If students fail to meet your expectations, you can put sanctions in place to deal with them.

5.  **Tell them exactly what you want and why you want it:** Some students fail to see what they are doing wrong or why they need to adjust their behaviour. Therefore, as the teacher you need to let them know exactly what they are doing wrong and the impact it is having. The student will then understand why what they are doing is not acceptable: the consequences or impacts are too great to be ignored. So instead of 'Stop talking', you say 'Stop talking, because when you talk it stops other students from learning, and that's not fair to them'. The instruction explains clearly what you want them to do, but also the reason why you want them to do it. It is the second part which is most powerful. Another powerful technique is to sometimes add emotion into the equation. 'Stop talking, because when you talk I feel frustrated, and it stops others from learning'.

6.  **Remind them of the good things:** Nothing disarms a student better than you saying that you like them. Watch as their faces change before your very eyes as you say it. This needs to be done during a one-to-one situation to have any resonance, whether this is a word in the corridor or during a detention. The point of it is to separate the student from the behaviour, so try to find something good to say about the student. I know this can be challenging at times, but it makes conflict resolution so much swifter and more efficient.

## Example scenario

'Susan, I'm going to talk first; then I will listen to what you have to say. I like you, Susan. I think you are a fantastic scientist and the work you did last lesson was brilliant, so I don't know why today you are talking over me. It stops me from giving out instructions and helping others, because I have to continually remind you to get on with the task, and that's not fair on the others. OK, it's your turn now.'

You can see that, by praising the student, aggressive or uncooperative behaviour will be minimised or even avoided, helping you to resolve the conflict more easily, rather than becoming involved in a long, drawn out episode that diverts you from teaching the class.

7. **Don't compromise on your expectations:** Just because you are trying to resolve conflict does not mean that you should neglect your standards. Bring the students' behaviour up to your standards; don't lower yourself to theirs. So when you are talking to them in the corridor or in a detention, don't settle for answers with poor attitude; disarm the student by saying, 'You are obviously not ready to discuss this sensibly or properly so I will give you a few moments to think about how we speak to each other'. Then walk away. This gives the student time to reflect on their behaviour and how they speak to you. After a minute or so, attempt to re-engage with the student. If they display the same poor attitude, then repeat the instruction above until they talk to you in a satisfactory manner. This may appear petty, but setting the standard of how you expect students to converse puts down a marker and reinforces your authority in the classroom.

8. **Follow the conventions of a conversation (you talk, they listen; they talk, you listen):** When dealing with conflict, set the guidelines for the conversation; these are the simple conventions of when one person is talking, the other listens. Remind the students of this to stop them from interrupting when you speak and then grant them the courtesy of listening to their retort. As with the point above, it sets your standard of behaviour and also reinforces your authority.

9. **Don't be distracted:** Deal with one behaviour incident at a time. Children are masters of trying to distract you away from the primary behaviour that needs to be addressed. Don't be suckered into diversionary tactics; remember to focus on why you are speaking to them in the first place.

10. **Don't sweat the small stuff:** In other words, pick your battles. This does not mean you have to compromise your standards; it means that you may choose to ignore a certain behaviour for the greater good of the class. For example, if a student in your class talks constantly and you have told him/her to listen, and now you have got them to listen but they are unknowingly tapping a pen, do you really want to stop the lesson again to deal with the pen? We all have our own standards and triggers, but I would suggest not every misdemeanour needs to be tackled if it is to the detriment of the learning taking place in the classroom.

11. **The beach ball effect:** Imagine that you and another person are holding a huge beach ball and you are asked the same question: 'What colour is the beach ball?' You may answer confidently 'red, white and blue' whilst the other person adamantly says 'orange, yellow and green'. Despite looking at the same ball, you see different colours; it depends on your perspective. This difference of perspective is important to recognise when trying to resolve conflict. It is always worthwhile trying to consider the student's perspective. There may be times when we jump to the wrong conclusions and make assumptions.

12. **Offer the students choice:** This, above all others, is the technique I feel has the greatest impact on conflict resolution and student behaviour. Offering the student a choice of how they respond to your instruction puts the power in their hands. Then they will either respond positively to your instruction or negatively, in which case you can apply the pre-discussed sanction or consequence. The student has chosen to respond and they cannot blame you for their decision.

## Example Scenarios:

Susan has produced little work and is talking to her friend.

'Susan, I can see that you have not produced a lot of work; either stop talking and get on with your work or I will move you to the front of the class. It's your choice.'

If Susan then continues to talk, you can move her to the front, and there will be less conflict because she was aware of the consequences, yet she chose to talk. If Susan then argues with you, you can state, 'You chose to talk; you knew the consequences.' In my experience, this often disarms the student; the instruction was clear and they made their own choice, creating their own outcome to the situation.

13. **Rewards:** Most schools operate a rewards system and these can be a good extrinsic motivator for many students. Whether it be for producing exceptional work or for excellent behaviour, rewards can help to motivate and engage students. One tip which works well with some students is to give the rewards from the previous lesson at the start of the current lesson. This can act as a motivator for the current lesson.

## Example scenario:

Previous lesson: 'Susan. your answer to question three was fantastic. and you produced a really accurate graph. Well done. Remind me to give you a credit next lesson.'

Current lesson: 'Susan, I owe you a credit, don't I, for your excellent work last lesson. Let's see if you can get another credit today by working as hard as last lesson.'

Holding back the reward reminds the student of what they did well last lesson that gained them the reward and reminds them that if they reproduce the same behaviours and effort, they can be successful again. Some students may need this prompt to help them engage with the lesson again to the same high level.

14. **Resolve issues:** If you have an issue with a particular student, or if they have failed to attend a detention, try to resolve these matters prior to your next lesson with that student. I know this is not always possible, but it stops problems dragging on or affecting subsequent lessons. I try to find students at break time or lunch to have a quick word about our next steps. This may be me issuing another detention or sitting down with the student for five minutes to explain why their behaviour last lesson was not acceptable. Whatever the discussion, it is far better held before the lesson so any issues can be resolved.

# Dealing with those hard-to-reach classes

Every so often a perfect storm of conditions comes along which creates a class that is harder to engage than others – that last lesson on a Friday just after the students have had drama. It can fill you with dread and you wait all week for it to be over. Below are a few techniques to steady the ship so that you can ensure high quality teaching and learning taking place against all the odds.

## Stage 1: Planning

I plan more for those hard-to-reach classes than for any other class I teach because they present far more challenge and barriers to learning than any other; therefore, I need to try to prepare for all situations I can expect to occur. Think carefully about how you will approach each phase of the lesson, from how the students enter the class to how they leave. For this class, more than any other, it is vital that I am there at the door to meet and greet. I may need to ask a few students to take a second to calm down before entering the classroom because they are still Very excitable from the previous drama lesson.

## Stage 2: Starter

I need this starter to be engaging and settling. I may choose from a repertoire of starters covered in the starter chapter or I may give the students a minute to read their work before they have a subject-specific spelling test. A spelling test is a great settler because it has to be conducted under quiet conditions and they need to listen carefully to the words. The words you use can then be written on the board as 'key words' to be referred to throughout the lesson and support the learning. Whichever starter I choose, it is important that it reinforces or consolidates learning. The starter needs to be clearly communicated, requiring little instruction, so I can deal with any issues at the start of the lesson and disruption is at a minimum.

## Stage 3: Chunking

For certain classes, the chunking of challenges is critical to ensure they stay on task and are able to complete the work to the desired standard. Chunking allows you to maintain the students' engagement whilst delivering a significant section of the course or topic. The best approach I have found for this is to produce a work booklet for the students to work through independently. It means that the students have all that is required during the lesson at their fingertips and disruption is minimised. The booklets are able to cover a number of key teaching and learning principles.

- They have success criteria that students can refer to whenever they want.

- The challenges are open ended and accessible to all students and yet contain elements of rigour and stretch.

- Students develop knowledge, understanding and skills through a series of progressively harder challenges.

- They allow the opportunity to develop cross curricular skills, including literacy and numeracy.

- They provide the opportunity to question students' understanding.

- Students are able to work independently.

- They contain extension challenges for those students who require it.

- They allow students who have been absent from a lesson to go back to complete work and therefore there are no gaps in the student's work, knowledge or understanding.

From a teacher's point of view, they are a fantastic medium to use to allow you to facilitate the learning taking place in your classroom. Work booklets require minimal instruction, and they give you the opportunity to support students one to one or in small groups as the remainder of the class proceed through the challenges.

## Stage 4: Questioning

Questioning is essential to discover how well the students are developing their knowledge and understanding of the topic. You may require students to go back in the booklet and then you instigate 5 minutes of silent reading as they digest the work that they have produced so far. This time also acts as revision for the test stage.

## Stage 5: Test/assess

At this stage, it is important to assess how well the students are progressing, and where the gaps in the learning exist, to inform your planning for next lesson. This may be achieved by a quick ten-question quiz or an exam question based on the content they have been learning. Whichever method you choose to test, feedback is necessary to help the students to improve their performance.

## Stage 6: Plenary for progress

Towards the end of the lesson, it is important to provide the opportunity for the students to reflect on what they have learned, and you may want them to summarise what they have learned and how they have learned it.

This simple formula for a lesson has helped me greatly with challenging classes. It requires a fair amount of work to design the booklet and set up, but once it is in place, it gives you the freedom to teach and support as the students work independently to complete the challenges. I introduce the lesson as a menu that I write on the board so that everyone knows what they have to do. I also set a minimum expectation for the class so each student knows, from the start of the lesson, what he/she is expected to complete before the end of the lesson. This helps to reduce conflict in the classroom: Students are fully aware of what they need to achieve and understand that if they fail to deliver, then they have to stay behind to complete it or come back for a detention.

**Lesson Menu**

1) Starter: Reflect and correct

2) Spelling test

3) Main course: Complete challenges 1–5 (MINIMUM)

4) Extension challenges 6–8

5) Dessert: Quiz time

6) I have progressed by . . .

## Dialogue to support

**Meet and greet:**

'Morning . . . you had a great lesson last time let's see if you can do it again.'

'Hello . . . how are you . . . the starter's on the board, you know what to do.'

'Morning . . . Mr Clark said you were brilliant in history; let's have a great lesson today.'

'Hello . . . I owe you a credit for that great writing you did last lesson.'

**Books/worksheet/equipment:**

'The page number for the book we will be using today is on the board; you can start to read it through in silence whilst I take the register.'

'Each row has ten worksheets to pass out. You have 20 seconds to hand them out. Go.'

**Effective instructions:**

'When I say *go*, I want one member from each group to come to the front and collect the equipment. Go.'

Dealing with conflict:

'Susan, do you understand that that behaviour is not appropriate in the classroom? What should you be doing?'

'Susan, you are talking again. What support do you need?'

'**When** you complete challenge three, **then** you can have a credit.'

'It's OK to feel frustrated and not OK to swear in the classroom.'

'What the rule on mobile phones?'

'Susan, I asked you to go outside because you have had three chances to make the right decision and you chose to ignore my instruction. Are you able to go back into the class and sit down without disrupting others and continue with the work?'

'Susan, you continue to ignore my instructions, so the choice is you go back in and sit at the front of the class and I will help you with your work or you can go and work in another classroom, your choice. If you choose to work in another class, we will have to repeat this part of the lesson. I will need to give you a detention so you don't fall behind.'

'Do you want some time to think?'

---

**Classroom management, in a nutshell**

- Planning is the key to classroom management. Design a seating plan that helps to reduce behavioural issues. Plan for those 'barriers to learning'.

- Establish clear routines that all students can adhere to.

- Remember, every lesson is new; try not to carry emotional baggage from one class to the next.

- Give clear and effective instructions; ask students to repeat them back to you so there are no misconceptions about what is expected.

- You must follow through on warnings.

- Isolate the behaviour from the student: It's not the student you don't like, it's their behaviour.

- Tell the students what you want and why you want it.

- Listen to what they have to say and try to see it from their point of view.

- Take a deep breath and remember that you are the adult.

**Figure 11.1** Classroom management, in a nutshell

# 12

# Marking for progress

I would say that for most teachers this is the one aspect of our work that we loathe. Nothing makes the heart sink faster than a pile of books waiting for our attention; it is even worse when it is a pile of books that you have taken home to mark, failed to mark, and the following morning find by the door still in the bag or in the huge plastic box you lug around everywhere. The irony is that the one thing we despise to do is seen as having one of the biggest positive impacts upon our students. Professor John Hattie states that feedback is one of the key influences that has the greatest effect on the success of our students. It is important to note at this point that what Hattie refers to as 'feedback' includes not only what we already regard as marking, but also the use of success criteria, so that students are aware of what they are going to be marked against. Regardless of any research, it should be clear to us that students receiving and acting on feedback is one of the most powerful strategies to achieving success. If we consider how we learn and get better at something, the process is as follows: We have a go, either we tell ourselves or people tell us what we need to do to improve, we follow the advice, learn from mistakes and we get better with more practice. Obvious, really. Therefore, if we know that feedback has one of the biggest influences on our students, why then is it all too often the forgotten task or the one duty that is low on the list of priorities? What can we do to look at marking and feedback in a new light, with a fresh approach?

One problem when discussing marking is that there are now so many terms used around this topic that it can be confusing knowing what people are actually talking about. There are a number of key words and phrases bandied about when referring to marking; all were fashionable at one time, but the three most common terms are *marking, feedback* and *assessment*. But what is the difference between the three? Well, for me, it is important to keep it simple:

Marking: This is the overall practice of ticking or crossing students' work with comments based on the work. Marking encompasses both feedback and assessment.

Feedback: The comments you make that are aimed at improving the student's performance.

Assessment: This is the grade/score/level you give to a student based upon set standards.

It is important to share these definitions with your staff, colleagues and students so that you all know what you are referring to during professional or learning conversations. Clarity is key to improving practice, both with staff and students.

So now we can define marking. What exactly are we marking and what are we marking for? When it comes to marking, we are generally addressing four key areas: the student's **knowledge and understanding** of the content in your subject; the **skills** they are developing within your subject, whether these are subject-specific or cross curricular such as literacy and numeracy; the **learning processes**, how they are learning and what skills they are utilising to learn; and then, finally, how well they have learned against set **criteria or standards.** Teachers' marking should therefore address these areas. It may be useful to share with students what aspect you are focusing on. For example, you may inform students that your marking this week will be focused on skills. Therefore, the feedback you give will concentrate on improving the skill performance of that student.

# How to develop a learning dialogue to improve student performance

## Target questions

This is a simple technique to improve a student's knowledge and understanding of a particular topic. Having marked the student's work, pose a specific question for the individual student to reflect on and answer. This question may be differentiated and can be based on what the student learned in the previous lesson/lessons, or it may be a precursor to what the students are about to learn. A target question based on a previous lesson is useful to re-engage the student with the topic: I would usually ask him/her to answer the question during the 'reflect and correct' time at the start of the lesson. It helps students to reflect on previous work and reminds them of what they did last lesson. The question may require the students to look back in their books and reread their notes; ideally, the students can recall the answer without using reference material, but looking back to remind themselves is a useful way to consolidate and apply their knowledge from previous lessons. The advantage for the teacher is that the question or questions may be the same for all students, to highlight any particular gaps in knowledge and understanding, or they may be differentiated to meet the needs of different students or groups of students.

The target question that is a precursor to the lesson allows the teacher to get a clear idea of what the students already know about the topic and where the gaps in learning may be. Target questions are a great way for students to demonstrate what they know and understand about the content of your subject. They provide you with a clear indication of misconceptions or gaps in knowledge, allowing you to adapt and tailor your teaching to meet those learning needs.

## Example of target questions

In the previous lesson, students had been learning about food chains in a biology lesson. The following three target questions could be used to assess the students' knowledge and understanding of that concept.

**(T)** What is a food chain?

**(T)** Can you list five primary producers to a food chain?

**(T)** Can you sketch a food chain showing four trophic levels?

There is obvious differentiation with these three questions, all tailored to meet the needs of your students; thus, students receive a more personalised marking service.

The next step is a brief class discussion on the answers to the questions, giving students the opportunity to amend and improve their responses. You may need to prompt students by asking them to add to their answers or correct their answers in order to improve them.

## I have progressed by . . .

This is an effective personal feedback device and, whether you use this technique midway through the lesson as a plenary or as a topic review, it serves as a great indicator of student progress. I simply ask the students to complete the sentence 'I have progressed by . . .'. You could ask for a minimum of six lines detailing how they have advanced or for the students to note down three key ideas they have developed. I may also ask them to reflect on the skills they have improved, not just the specific subject content. It allows the students an opportunity to consider what they have learned and how they have learned it. If you ask students to go back and read their 'I have progressed by . . .' comments, they find stepping stones to link up their work from lesson to lesson. These statements give you the opportunity to check students' understanding and skill development, as well as highlight any misconceptions that you can rectify in future lessons.

## Feedback

This is the mainstay of marking for progress, and it involves several key components. The impact when carried out consistently can be astonishing.

## Stage 1

Success criteria: This defines what success looks like and clarifies to students what they will be judged or marked against. For the teacher, it provides an explicit set of standards to look for. It helps you to be concise with your feedback, diagnosing where the problems/ issues may be and therefore what can be done to remedy them. Sharing the success criteria with students is critical to the marking process and thus the improved performance of the students. Success criteria can be shared with the students at the start of the activity so that they know what they are aiming for, or it may be held back (for example, during a lesson that involves a test). In either case, success criteria is the building blocks for progress as they show well-defined steps that need to be taken in order to improve and progress. The success criteria may be used to assign the students a grade score or level, depending on how you want to use it. If you do grade or score the work, it has been suggested that you keep your feedback comments to a minimum because students will only concentrate on the grade, rather than the comment. However, as long as you spend sufficient time allowing students to reflect on their grade, I think a feedback comment at this point is the perfect opportunity for students to consider how they can improve their performance.

## Stage 2

Self-assessment: Asking the students to assess their own performance develops their awareness of success criteria and what they need to do in order to be successful. This self-reflection gives the students ownership of the marking process and fosters 'response-ability' as they become self-aware of the steps necessary in order to progress. The key to outstanding self-assessment is the quality of the question you pose to the students, as mentioned previously:

Questions require answers.

Answers demand thought.

Thought creates decision.

Decision inspires positive action.

The following questions are useful to get the students to reflect on their work. It is important to help students to develop their learning vocabulary when faced with these questions. Rather than the students answering with 'I found it hard' or 'I got stuck', support students to look more deeply and dissect the problems – for example 'I found it hard because I hadn't drawn my graph accurately' or 'I got stuck because I did not use the formula provided'. This self-reflection can then be used to set targets for the next time you set up a similar activity. 'Target: Take time and check the points of the graph are drawn correctly' or 'Use the formula provided when calculating'.

- On a scale of one to ten, how would you rate today's work? Why?

- Which part of your work are you most pleased with?

- Which part of the work was most challenging? Why?

- What would you do differently next time?

- What could you do to improve your performance?

- What grade/score/level would you say you are working at? Why?

- What went well (WWW)? Even better if (EBI)?

- Medal and mission statements

## Stage 3

*Comment*

I always begin my written comments by using the student's name; it makes my marking personal to him/her rather than a blanket statement to all students. I follow this up with specific praise related to the student's work in his/her book or performance in the class-room. It is far more powerful to give precise praise rather than an overall general comment: 'A well labelled diagram, well done' is far better than 'Good work'. 'Good work': What was good about it? Which part was good? Those comments are too ambiguous; if you are specific in your praise, students are more likely to replicate the good aspects time and time again to improve their work and seek your appreciation once more.

## Stage 4

*Feedback/targets to improve*

Feedback talks about what the student did, and discusses what the student can do next time in order to improve performance. In order for feedback to be useful, it must refer to the success criteria – in other words, 'you got this' because 'you did that'. It is the next part that is so important and what all outstanding marking hinges on. Feedback on what the student needs to do to improve performance is what is of key importance. We must support students to unlock their future potential rather than dwell on their past performance. This feature of marking should be positive and specific; it may refer to the success criteria or it may be a specific target you want the student to work on. Either way it must be actioned by the student for progress to be made.

As part of this process, I may ask the students to highlight key aspects of their work I wanted them to focus on. This may be based upon previous feedback I have given the students. Therefore, at the start of the piece of work I will have asked them to look back at their previous targets and state that I want them to action them during this lesson. For example, I may ask them to do one or more of the following:

- Highlight where you think you have met the 'mastery' criteria.

- Highlight where you have used capital letters for names and places.

- Highlight where you have linked ideas.

- Highlight where you have used connectives.

## Stage 5

*Spelling, punctuation and grammar (SPAG)*

Your school may have a specific marking policy for spelling, punctuation and grammar, and it is therefore necessary for you to follow their guidelines. If students' SPAG is never corrected then how are they ever going to improve? My focus will always be on subject-specific words and I look to correct commonly misspelt words, as well. As a general rule, I will correct five or six spelling mistakes, enough for the student to correct without the task becoming too onerous or demoralising. I ask students to write out the correct spellings three times, and if it is a common mistake, I may discuss it with the class as a whole, using one of the three spelling techniques covered in the chapter on literacy for learning.

## Stage 6

*Action targets (reflect and correct)*

Your action targets should be based around the specific nuts and bolts of the students' work – in other words, those targets that, if achieved by the student, would have the greatest impact upon their performance. It is important that the target or targets are realistic and clearly understood by the student. In my experience if your targets are short and sweet, they are more likely to be actioned. For example, asking a student to rewrite his/her essay using more connectives is unlikely to inspire the student to complete the task; however, asking a student to rewrite a paragraph using five connectives from the literacy mat – now that is achievable. Rather than setting a number of targets that are unlikely to be undertaken it is worth considering setting just one target. It is the accumulation of all those incremental improvements that will have a decisive improvement on student performance when it matters. Below are three target stems I use that are nonjudgemental and nonthreatening to a student's self-esteem and confidence.

Next time . . .

Practise . . .

Try this . . .

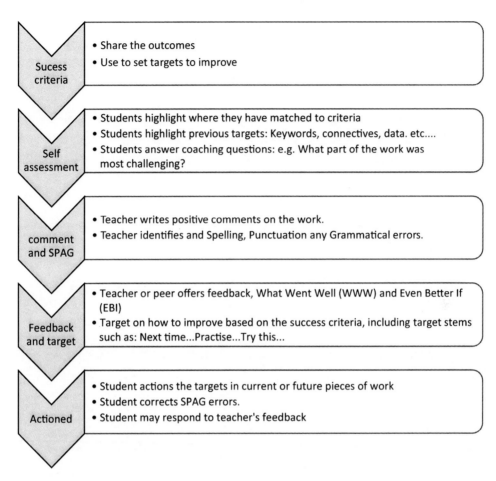

**Figure 12.1** The marking process

As a teacher, if you have noticed a learning need, you must build in an opportunity to revisit that challenge. Targets you set do not have to be actioned there and then in the lesson. It may be that you will not be revisiting a specific skill set for a few weeks, in which case ask students to look back in their books so that they can remind themselves of the specific target you require them to work on. I get my students to highlight where they have actioned their target so that it is clear for me to see that they have reflected on the feedback and improved their performance.

## Marking devices to improve student progress

### How to use model work when marking

If you want your students to improve their performance, use model work when marking and returning students' work. For some key skills, I select the best example I can find in the class and photocopy it for all the other students. They then stick this in their books and we annotate around the example to focus on the aspects of the work that make it excellent.

## Use pre-prepared marking grids

These can be a useful time saving device and they structure your marking and self/peer assessment. Construct marking grids that provide the students with not only the success criteria but also opportunity to reflect on their own learning and identify ways to improve.

Table 12.1 shows an exam for music.

**Table 12.1**   Music marking grid

**How do I compose a reggae song?**

Target to improve:

| Developing | Secure | Enhanced/mastery |
|---|---|---|
| • Structure: chorus **or** verse<br>• Reggae keyboard style<br>• Given chord sequence with two chords<br>(No melody or bass) | • Structure: intro – chorus **or** verse – coda<br>• Reggae keyboard style<br>• Given chord sequence with two chords. Off-beat chords.<br>• Bass on beats 1 and 3<br>Melody that fits with the chords (vocal or instrumental) | • Structure: intro – chorus **and** verses – coda<br>• Two contrasting chord sequences (given)<br>• Some more complex rhythms in the bass and/or chords<br>• Lyrics with a serious message which fit in with the rhythm<br>Percussion instruments<br>• Structure includes an instrumental break<br>Sections are **developed** on repeats with e.g. countermelody, accompanying rhythms varied, another part added |

• Highlight where you think you have matched the success criteria
• Highlight in another colour your one target to improve on next time.

Self-assessment: What Went Well (WWW)


Feedback: What could you do to improve/ Even Better If (EBI)


Teacher feedback:


Response to teacher feedback:

## Use pre-prepared feedback sheets

Having a bank of targets for students to action allows you to highlight the most appropriate target on the sheet that applies to the student at that time. This can help to speed up the marking process, and students receive targets specific to their learning need.

Examples of generic target statements:

- Practise using key words in your written responses.

- Try using evidence to back up your statements; this will help you secure more marks in the exam.

- Create a series of flashcards to help you remember the key points on the topic.

- Try writing the question in the answer; it will help you to stay on track and structure your response. For example: Question: What was the distribution of Vikings within Europe? Answer: The distribution of Vikings within Europe were mainly concentrated in the northern Scandinavian countries, including Sweden, Norway and Denmark.

- Try using the success criteria when you write your answers; it will help guide you to better work.

- Practise underlining the command words in questions so you are clear on what you need to do.

- Practise linking ideas together by using connectives: *in addition, therefore, because, also.*

## Verbal Feedback

When you are discussing a student's work with them or informing the class on ways in which they can improve their work, ask them to record this verbal feedback by writing down the key points. This way it acts as a record for the student to refer back to when they need to. Students write VF for verbal feedback in the margin of the book to be used as a reference point for the future.

---

**Marking for progress, in a nutshell**

- Feedback is one of the most important devices to improve students' performance.

- Set target questions for students to action. Differentiate these questions to add additional challenge.

- Use success criteria for summative assessment and to set the next steps for progress.

- Ensure students action targets.

**Figure 12.2**   Marking for progress, in a nutshell

# 13

# How to get students to remember what you teach them

Part of being an outstanding teacher is providing students with the necessary knowledge, understanding and skills to be able to achieve their own goals and targets. For many students, their long term goal will be to achieve aspirational examination results, gaining success and allowing them to go on to further their career. I always feel that exams are a bit of a paradox: They are designed to test the culmination of years of work and yet they assess what you know on one day at one moment in time. So the challenge as teachers is for us to embed knowledge and ingrain skills into our students' practice over the years so that they can perform on that one day.

If we want students to be successful and ready to meet the rigours of examinations and modern life, then we cannot merely teach them content that they repeat verbatim in an exam, without really understanding it. They cannot just regurgitate facts and figures and hope they relate to the question. We are preparing 21st-century learners, and modern examinations demand that they are resourceful, flexible, responsive and tenacious. Not only examinations demand these skills – these are what the world of work is crying out for.

## It begins on day one

One trait many outstanding teachers share is total clarity on their goal. They are clear about what they want to achieve and know which steps they need to follow in order to achieve it. For most teachers, the primary aim is to support students to help them realise their potential and achieve aspirational targets; in addition, they nurture those social skills that enable the students to be competent and confident individuals, teaching their students the necessary skills to be successful in later life. To break this down further, many outstanding teachers have the goal to ensure that every student they teach gains his/her aspirational target grade or score in the exam. They know that this does not begin weeks or months before the exam but rather on the first day at the school.

Every lesson counts; therefore, every lesson has to have a clear purpose; even in the very first lesson you have with a class, you should consider: What is it for? What are you hoping that the students will learn? The aim of the lesson should be related to the long term goal of enabling your students to achieve the aspirational grades or scores in five or seven years' time. I know curricula can change and subject content may alter, but the foundations and skills will remain the same: how to add up; how to read music; how to write an excellent answer in your subject; how to link ideas together; how to speak, read and write like a historian, scientist or artist. These skills don't change nor are they learned in a few lessons. They are nurtured, practised and mastered over years of instruction, feedback, reflection and dedication. Thus, if you want your students to be outstanding and gain outstanding results, you must yourself think about outstanding and plan for outstanding from day one.

Having discussed the importance of making every lesson count from day one, we can focus on the trick of making sure students remember what you have taught them and are able to apply it years down the line when they sit their exams. Maybe a good place to start is to first investigate why we forget.

Why is it that we forget names at parties or in social situations? Within school it can often be new students names that pose the problem, let's consider our new class. It can be difficult to remember all the names because we are overloaded with information and our brain is trying to process a lot all at once. Not only remembering names, but giving out books, sorting out a seating plan, dealing with behaviour – it's a lot to take on board so our brain prioritises our actions, deciding that it is more important to remember to give out equipment than to remember a student's name. However, the names you remember are often those students who have older siblings at the school, or those who have an unusual name, or a name of somebody else you know. These names offer you a connection, and the brain loves to make connections.

Going back to why we forget names at parties: One theory is that because it is a social situation, we are more relaxed and therefore less inclined to concentrate on cementing names into our longer term memory. Another reason for forgetting is explained by decay theory. This is the concept that, over time, if we do not use the information we have learned, then it will begin to fade from our minds. It is generally accepted that we can retain about seven pieces of information in our short term memory, and then if this is not transferred across to our long term memory, the information is lost.

So the key points on why we forget are:

1.    Distraction: We are trying to do too much at once.

2.    Relaxed state: We are too relaxed to retain information.

3.    Connections: We fail to make connections between pieces of information.

4.    Decay: Our information fades if we do not use it.

5.  Transfer: If we make no attempt to do something with the information to embed it into our long term memory, then it will fade.

So having considered why we forget, all we have to do is tackle each of the components above with our students. Then they will remember everything we teach them and pass their exams with flying colours. Easy! Ha!

# How to learn anything

Anything can be learned. It's just a case of applying a few simple principles supported by practice and held together with motivation.

## Stage 1

**What do you want them to know and why?** This may seem an obvious question, but it is important to have clarity on this point. You must be clear yourself as to what you are trying to achieve in the lesson. Ask yourself, what do I want the student to know? And why is it important to teach it? As long as you are happy with your own answer to these two questions, then all is well and good. However, if you are struggling to establish the reason why you are teaching a particular aspect of your subject, then you must go back and consider the importance of your lesson. How could you make it more relevant to the students? How could it be improved to meet their needs? What are you intending that the students gain from your lesson? If you really want to challenge your own thinking, consider which areas of knowledge and /or skills you would prioritise for the students if the exam were in a month's time. This is a useful question to fix your thinking on the most important aspects of your course. It helps you to prioritise what you teach and also focuses your teaching, thus reducing 'filler' lessons.

## Stage 2

**Deconstruct the knowledge or skill:** Break down what you want the students to learn into component parts. Create a series of stages or steps to follow makes the whole subject or topic far more manageable for the students. For example, instead of saying 'Today we will be working on our French speaking', break that down to 'Today we are going to learn how to order food at a French restaurant' – instantly more specific and accessible for the students. Don't try to do too much at once: Focus on embedding one skill at a time until it is mastered and automatic. Therefore, for the challenge above, the teacher may see more benefit and mastery from the students by just focusing on one appropriate conversation starter (for example, how to order drinks from a menu, rather than trying to get all students to be able to competently hold a conversation with a French waiter whilst ordering drinks, starters, and main courses; chatting about the weather; and asking for the bill). Share this process with the students, explaining how you will be dissecting the course content and describing the process so that they can see the whole picture and understand how it all fits together. Students will see progression and have increased confidence in the process. It also ensures that no one gets left behind.

## Stage 3

**Consolidation:** You have to do something with what you have learned; this reduces memory decay. It's the adage 'use it or lose it'! Having learned the subject content or skill, students who do not reflect on or use it will often forget it. Many a time I have been faced with a class that appears to have no recollection of the previous lesson or maybe only remembering an insignificant moment – for example, that I tripped or that Susan fell off her chair. However, that begs the question, why do the students remember those seemingly insignificant moments? Part of the reason may be that if you want students to consolidate information, then you must try to include a number of memory cues. In the examples above, it was 'action' that created the memory: I tripped or Susan fell, both physical actions that lead to a connection in the mind between the lesson and me tripping/ Susan falling. There are a number of cues you can use to aid memory:

Action: Get the students moving to help them remember; associate information with actions (for example, punctuation Kung Fu is widely used in primary schools). Create silly hand gestures or handshakes to remember key facts.

Bizarre: Make your explanations and associations bizarre and outrageous – the more outrageous the better. The brain loves extremes, so creating weird and wonderful images in the students' minds can serve as a great retainer of information.

Place: Relate information to places or locations the students knows well. Take the students on a tour of the school, stopping at various points to teach part of your course. Then recant the route back in the classroom, asking students to recite what they remember from the various locations you stopped at.

Senses: Use a range of senses to engage students' thinking. Ask them to feel the soil rather than read about it, smell the coffee rather than imagine. The more senses you can engage the better.

Colourful: Ask students to add colour to their work, or highlight it to make it more memorable.

Linked: Link ideas together to build associations in the mind.

Sequence: Sequence information in clear steps or stages to help students recall.

Explicit: Students remember the explicit well.

'Without immediate, then regular, review of new information, recall can drop by as much as 80% within 24 hours' (Alistair Smith, *Accelerated Learning in the Classroom*, 1996).

## Stage 4

**Application:** This is the stage where students can demonstrate what they have learned. Having learned the new content or skill, they need time to apply it. This may be in the form of a paper, a quiz or a short test. Whichever system you use, it is vital that students are given the opportunity to apply their newfound skill or knowledge. To improve recall, best practice is to have students apply themselves in the short, medium and long term. This can be achieved by:

- A short quiz or test at the end of the lesson based on the content they have just been learning.

- A short quiz at the start of the following lesson will test how much information the students have consolidated in the short term.

- An exam after several weeks have passed will assess the students' long term memory and just how well they can apply the knowledge and skill they have previously learned.

This simple three-stage approach has been very successful with my exam classes over the years. The short quizzes may only be 7–10 questions, requiring one word answers or short responses, but they have helped to consolidate learning very well. It is that constant drip feeding and recall of information that helps students to ingrain the knowledge.

## Stage 5

**Feedback and practice:** Once students have had the chance to demonstrate what they have learned, then it is imperative to give feedback on what went well and what the student needs to do to get better. Then the student must practise, revisiting each stage again as necessary. Again, it is important to deconstruct the knowledge or skill: Feedback such as 'Revise your notes' does little to impact upon the students learning. Far better to say 'Read through your notes and highlight the key points' since this gives some guidance on how the student can relate their notes to the several consolidation cues mentioned previously. I often stress to my students that the lesson when they sat the practice test was not the important one; it is the feedback lesson that is the important one. It's the lesson where they discover what they can do to improve that is crucial, not the lesson when they sat in silence. When giving feedback, ask the students, 'How did you remember that?' or 'Can we come up with a way to remember that?' These two questions can create some insightful answers that benefit the whole class.

## Memory devices

**Cornell notes:** This idea is attributed to Cornell University in America. It is a note taking system that involves active learning rather than just copying down chunks of information or text. You may provide students with templates or simply ask them to divide up their page into several sections.

Table 13.2 shows an adapted version I use with my class.

To embed this knowledge, students are given time during the lesson to teach each other what that have learned. They can share their ideas and discuss their notes. Which key words have they selected? How do their summaries differ? And so on. Students are then instructed to read through their notes again and make any amendments (consolidation). These notes are then reviewed during the following lesson – this may be a short quiz or

**Table 13.1** Cornell notes template

| Title: | |
|---|---|
| Key questions: | Main points: <br> • Important dates/times/places <br> • Topic headers <br> • Diagrams/pictures/tables/graphs <br> • Formulas <br> • Stages of a process |
| Summary: | |

**Table 13.2** Adapted Cornell notes template

| Learning Question: | | |
|---|---|---|
| Questions to support: | Main points (prioritised): | Key words: |
| | | |
| Summary: | | |
| Answer to the learning question: | | |

test (application). As mentioned previously, students are given the opportunity to apply what they have learned, and feedback is given.

**Head, shoulders, knees and toes:** This is a popular memory device with my students. Simply, we attach pieces of information to body parts, using the childhood song of 'Head, shoulders, knees and toes'. This allows you to assign eight pieces of information, not forgetting to include the eyes, ears, mouth and nose! Students stand up and perform the actions whilst substituting the body part for a key word or phrase you are teaching.

For example: The Water Cycle

Head: Evaporation

Shoulders: Condensation

Knees: Transpiration

Toes: Precipitation

Eyes: Surface run-off

Ears: Through-flow

Mouth: Infiltration

Nose: Interception

This device does not have to be limited to just the one song. Ask the students to replace the lyrics of their favourite songs for key words for your topic or subject. Adding in a choreographed dance routine makes it all the more memorable.

**Graffiti:** Students are given felt tip pens or board markers and allowed to write or draw all over their desks. They tend to really enjoy this activity as it feels like they are breaking the rules, and it has worked wonders with my low ability boys. You can set up parameters to which you want the students to work; for example, 'you can draw only three pictures', 'you must get down at least five key words', 'you must explain the process'. The students are given the opportunity to walk around the class and see what other students have produced and then given the opportunity to add to theirs. I then allow my students to take a photo of the desk using their phones, on the premise that they are far more likely to look at it again and they have a record of the work they have produced. A follow up homework may involve putting the information from the photo into more conventional notes (consolidation). If you don't have adequate desks, then old wall paper or backing paper works just as well.

**The peg system:** This is by far the most popular and successful memory technique with my students. It is a version of Tony Buzan's linked memory system (from *Use Your Memory*, 2003). When I first introduce this idea, the students think I've gone nuts and they can't see how it will help them. Then, as we work through the process, they are amazed at how much information they have retained.

This technique is a link association system or a number shape system that enables students to recall ten pieces of information. Information is 'pegged' onto numbers, then that information is retained by creating a story about that number.

## Stage 1

**The importance of Imagination:** It is important to emphasise to the students that they must be open minded to the ideas you are about to discuss. Also they must try to be as imaginative as possible: The bigger, bolder and more colourful the images they create in their minds the better. Visualise the images, imagine you were there; all this creativity creates stronger associations in the brain.

## Stage 2

**Create images for numbers one to ten:** The first thing students need to do is to replace the numbers one to ten with an image. You can ask 'What do you think number 1 looks like?' Then you work your way through to number ten, asking them what each number conjures up for them. The more successful systems are created individually by the student, and I often set homework challenges to create their own peg systems; however, for the sake of an example I create a class peg system taking suggestions from the students, and we agree on which images we prefer to use.

Below is a list of examples that students often use:

1   A pole, a man, a soldier, a pen, a paintbrush

2   Swan, duck

3   Boobs, bottom, mountain

4   Yacht, boat, table

5   Snake, hosepipe

6   Golf club, lasso

7   Bus shelter, boomerang, crocodile

8   Snowman, fat man

9   Giraffe, flag, sperm, tadpole

10  Thin man and a fat man, knife and a plate

## Stage 3

**Select ten pieces of information:** Having created your 'pegs', now it is necessary to select the information you wish to remember. To do this, I give the students a piece of text that they need to know for their exam, and I then ask the students to decide on the ten most important key ideas to bullet point. It is important that these points are succinct and brief. We then discuss as a class what we consider to be the top ten points, and I write these on the board.

## Stage 4

**Making the links and creating your story:** Having selected the ten key points, these are then 'pegged' onto the numbers by creating an imaginative story to link the two together.

## Stage 5

**Visualisation:** Once the story is created, I ask the students to close their eyes as I retell the story. After this, I question students on what each number represents (consolidation).

Once we, as a class, have discussed all ten points, I emphasise the importance of students trying to recall all the points again within the next 24 hours, to help consolidate the learning. Then the next time I see the students, we start off by testing what we can remember (application).

**An example: Ten facts on Vincent Van Gogh**

1) He was a post-impressionist painter.

2) He left school aged 15.

3) His painting 'Irises' sold for $54 million.

4) He moved to London in 1873.

5) He spoke four different languages: French, German, English and Dutch.

6) He was sacked from his job in London working at an art gallery.

7) He returned to Holland to become a minister.

8) He suffered with mental illness and cut off his ear.

9) One of his most famous paintings was 'Sunflowers'.

10) He died after shooting himself in the chest.

Now having created the ten facts we want to learn about Van Gogh, we need to apply the 'peg system' as described below.

1) (Paintbrush) Imagine a postman/woman doing an impression of a painter with a paint brush; this symbolises a post-impressionist painter.

2) (Swan) Imagine a swan with a mortar board on its head with fifteen signets following on behind.

3) Imagine a famous woman model with a boob job that cost $54 million and she is holding a bunch of irises.

4) Imagine Van Gogh at the front of a yacht in a 'Titanic' pose. The name of the yacht is London 1873.

5) Imagine a snake wearing a beret and clogs eating a large sausage whilst waving the Union Jack flag. (Stereotypical images, I'm afraid, but they work, even if snakes have no feet to wear clogs!)

6) Imagine Van Gogh being hit up the bottom by the golf club, symbolising him being sacked.

7) Imagine Van Gogh wearing a minister's dog collar and throwing a boomerang that reaches London then returns back to him in Holland.

8) Imagine a snowman with its ear cut off.

9) Imagine a herd of giraffes wandering through a field of sunflowers.

10) Imagine a thin man shooting a fat man in the chest.

I realise that this may sound like a gimmick and a bit bizarre. However, as I said it has worked wonders with students and I have found that the more bizarre and creative the ideas, the more successful the students have been in retaining the information. I appreciate that asking your students to close their eyes and visualise a snake wearing a beret is a bit strange, but give it a go. What have you got to lose?

### Roman rooms

Roman rooms, Sherlock Holmes's mind palace, the room system, all these are the same techniques under different guises. This device is the one used most often by memory champions the world over. It involves associating the information you want to learn to rooms within a house.

For me this has worked best by asking students to imagine their own house and I apply the premise that they all have a similar number of rooms. Obviously, each student's circumstances are different and therefore I stress to the students that because I will be using a set number of rooms, they may have to imagine rooms if they do not have them or if the layout of the house is very different.

The simple notion is that students imagine their house and they associate different rooms with different pieces of information that they are attempting to remember. However, as before, to make this device successful, they must make the association as big, bold and bizarre as possible. To help you to understand how this works I will use the example of attempting to remember the wives of Henry the VIII.

First I consider the rooms in the house.

**Table 13.3**   Roman rooms

| Room 1<br>(Hall) | Room 2<br>(Living room) |
|---|---|
| Room 3<br>(Kitchen) | Room 4<br>(Bathroom) |
| Room 5<br>(Bedroom 1) | Room 6<br>(Bedroom 2) |

Having divided up the house into six rooms, I then link each of Henry's wives to a room.

| Room 1<br>(Hall)<br>**Catherine of Aragon** | Room 2<br>(Living room)<br>**Anne Boleyn** |
|---|---|
| Room 3<br>(Kitchen)<br>Jane Seymour | Room 4<br>(Bathroom)<br>Anne of Cleves |
| Room 5<br>(Bedroom 1)<br>Catherine Howard | Room 6<br>(Bedroom 2)<br>Catherine Parr |

I then ask the students to close their eyes as I tell them the following story. I ask them to imagine they are walking around their house and to create an image in their mind to link a wife to each room.

As I enter the house, I see a naked woman who is standing with an arrogant look on her face and with a large sign around her neck that says 'Catherine' on it. This represents Catherine of Aragon (arrogant).

I then walk through to the living room where a headless woman is rolling her own head down a bowling alley. This symbolises Anne Boleyn (Bowlin') (as she was also beheaded).

In the kitchen are Tarzan and Jane who are cooking. There is so much smoke that Jane holds a pair of binoculars to her eyes so she can 'see more'. This depicts Jane Seymour, Henry's third wife.

In the bathroom a woman is in the shower with a meat cleaver, representing Anne of Cleves.

In bedroom 1 is a huge Catherine wheel firework which is spinning and sets fire to a pile of wood. This symbolises Catherine Howard (wood).

In bedroom 2 is a woman golfer who is putting for par, and on her golf bag is the name Catherine. This represents Catherine Parr.

Try it out yourself: Imagine the story and rooms above, and then test yourself on it tomorrow and see if you are impressed with the results. I am confident you will be.

Once you have demonstrated these techniques to the students, they can use them themselves to create their own 'mind palace' of information. The huge advantage of this technique is that it does not need to be limited to six pieces of information. You can use outside the

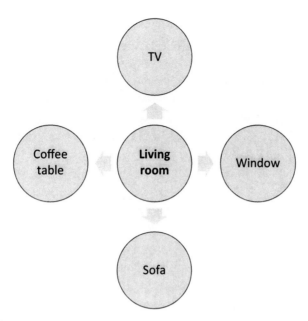

**Figure 13.1**  Additional Roman rooms

house, the front door, the stairs and even the garden. To take this device to the next level, you can then use items and features of each room to associate with more information (for example, within the living room you may link one idea to the sofa, another to the coffee table).

This dramatically increases the amount of information you can recall once it is linked to items. It just requires a creative imagination to conjure up ideas to associate information together.

So, for example, in the living room there could be worms crawling across the coffee table, birds tweeting on the window sill, a fox sitting on the sofa watching a documentary on badgers – all to help you to remember components of a food web for Biology. The potential is endless and only bound by your own imagination.

**Mnemonics:** I am sure we have all used mnemonics in the past to help us to remember. Richard of York Gave Battle In Vain to remember the colours of the rainbow, Red, Orange, Yellow, Green, Blue, Indigo and Violet. Or Naught Elephants Squirt Water for the compass direction, North, East, South, West. Whichever way we have used them, they are a powerful tool to aid recall. Rather than you having to create them all the time, challenge your students to devise their own mnemonics for key aspects of your course. These can then be shared with the class in future lessons. Again, remember: The more outrageous the better!

**Teach it:** If you really want students to have a deep understanding of your subject, get them to teach it to each other. There is no greater test of a student's understanding than having to teach what they have learned to others. This can be achieved in a number of ways: You may want all students to learn and teach each other the same aspects of the course, or you may want to differentiate the challenge. At the beginning of a new topic, divide the content and/or skills up into a number of key components. Then assign a student or groups of students one of those components to teach the others.

I put learning questions or content titles into a hat and get students to pick the topic they will need to research and teach the others about. This has worked well for me, but you may need to select the topics for individual groups depending upon the content, skills and the ability of the students.

**Foldables:** This is a useful device developed by Dinah Zike requiring students to consolidate their learning. Having learned about a particular topic I ask students to produce a 'foldable' on that work. These can be as creative and colourful as possible, and they involves students having to synthesise what they have been working on, prioritise what they consider to be most important and then organise information in a creative way. The information is displayed in a number of ways, using folded paper or card. Use the paper or card to make booklets, standing displays or, as I have done, ask the students to design and create their very own revision hats, wonderful creations with all the important information stored on them.

**Mind maps:** These were first developed by Tony Buzan in the 1960s. They are a powerful technique to develop links and connections within the brain. They enable students to make links between different ideas or components of your subject, organising them along a number of 'branches'. To be useful to students, they need to be more than just a spider diagram. It is important to combine words with pictures and to organise the information whilst making connections.

1) In the centre of the page, draw or use a picture to represent what it is you want to learn.

2) Connect your main branches to the central idea. Use different colours for each branch as this will help with recall.

3) From those main branches, you can draw subsequent branches connecting each with a single word or key phrase. Link ideas by making associations between pictures and words.

4) Make the whole map as colourful and creative as possible. As previously mentioned, the more creative you can be the easier and more likely it is that you will remember.

Mind maps are very useful when revising or reviewing a topic as they allow students to condense a mass of information into a single page.

**Past papers:** This is hardly a revolutionary idea but the benefit of using past papers to improve student performance cannot be overlooked. Just as an athlete creates muscle memory from repeatedly performing the same movement, so too can you develop memory from repetition. Practicing past papers questions gives students the opportunity to apply their learning within an exam scenario – the very conditions you are trying to replicate for their real exam day. This application phase is vital to cementing the students' learning and also to highlight any gaps in their knowledge or skill set. Past papers should be used in unison with the mark scheme because this serves as the success criteria, and therefore indicates how the student is performing and what they may need to do to improve. I also present the students with the examiner's report because this is a valuable resource that informs both the teacher and students of how the exam question was marked. It tells the students what common mistakes were made and informs the teachers of what needs to be included to make the exam responses better. Reviewing the examiner's report is great way to improve your teaching approach for certain aspects of the course and also useful to the student as they learn what mistakes not to make and how to improve their exam responses.

## Dialogue to support

'What you learn today, you could be tested on in two years' time, which is why it is so important to concentrate. But don't just listen, don't be a passive learner; get involved, ask questions, think deeply and review everything we do within 24 hours.'

'You can learn anything: You have exactly the same number of brain cells as all the greatest people you can think of. It's all about setting yourself goals, lots of practice, staying motivated and acting on feedback so you can achieve all you want in life.'

'The brain loves links, so link words to pictures, be creative! When you think of a word or phrase, associate it with an image – it's what all the great memory experts do'.

'Get curious, ask questions and explore the subject to discover the answers to questions you may have.'

---

**How to get students to remember what you teach them, in a nutshell**

- Every lesson counts: Each lesson must be linked to the greater long term goal of achieving success for the students.

- Make the lessons purposeful and don't try to do too much. Deconstruct the skill. If it's important, it needs mastering. Take time to ensure they have got it.

- Use it or lose it! Consolidate the learning; then apply the learning.

- To aid recall, spend time going over what you have learned in previous lessons. This helps students to reflect and consolidate their learning.

- Be creative and use your imagination. The key to memory techniques is creating big, bold, bizarre images in your head in weird and grand situations.

**Figure 13.2**  How to get students to remember what you teach them, in a nutshell

# 14
# How to create a culture of creativity and curiosity

In 2006 Sir Ken Robinson gave a speech as part of a TED Talk conference entitled 'Do Schools Kill Creativity?' It has become the most viewed TED Talk of all time with in excess of eight and a half million views currently. I believe its popularity is the result of both the content and also the excellent delivery by Sir Ken himself. It sometimes feels to me that creativity is often a sidelined feature of teaching – yet, in fact, it is a key element of education because it is the gateway to higher thinking. It allows students to develop their curiosity and explore their own learning.

The feeling that creativity is a forgotten aspect of teaching is a result of the current education system we operate in. With such drive to meet and exceed standards, teachers naturally look for the best way to impart knowledge and skills to enable their students to be successful. The problem is that many teachers believe that the best and quickest way to achieve this is by telling students what they need to know and expecting them to go away and learn it. It sometimes feels to me that teaching practice has become more of a science than an art. Review the data, apply sound teaching methods, test and assess and then repeat. It all feels very clinical. I understand why we all do it; there is tremendous pressure to cover all the content of the course, prepare students sufficiently for the exams and exceed targets. When have we got time to develop creativity or allow students to be curious? However, the reality is that creativity and curiosity are the very things that help to build understanding skills and memory. Which, in turn, will result in improved performance and achievement. As I have previously mentioned, learning is often:

Messy to begin with – frustrating in the middle – glorious at the end.

Curiosity in students creates a desire to learn, an intrinsic motivation to discover and explore. Curiosity is also a critical component of creativity and these two, hand in hand, can inspire your students to peak performance.

Please do not assume that I think that the education system is totally floored or that data has crushed creativity. I see a lot of merit in data and I am fine with teaching being considered a science. Yet there is a frustration when we feel limited in expressing our own creativity or restricted from nurturing that creativity and curiosity within our students.

## How to create a creative and curious culture within your classroom

If you want to create a creative and curious culture within your classroom, there are a number of key conditions to promote and support:

- Allow students to develop their own ideas.

- Ask questions that stimulate curiosity.

- Take risks.

- Test and try things out.

- Accept failure as a norm: Be prepared to be wrong.

- Learn from mistakes.

- Generate new ideas.

- Look at things from alternative angles.

- Research and make connections.

Beyond these conditions that can foster creativity and curiosity, there are also a number of strategies that can be used:

1) Learning questions: As mentioned in the chapter on planning, using a learning question as your lesson title is far more likely to create curiosity and wonder than a bland title. Ask students to comment on the question or to predict what they think the answer will be. The lesson is then based on discovery and exploration to answer the question.

2) What's in the box: I have a box with a hole in it, and I ask students to come to the front of the class and place their hand in the box to feel what is inside. The contents will most often be an item related to the answer to the learning question. Then, as the lesson proceeds, you may ask other students to have a go until they are able to relate the item in the box to the answer for the learning question.

3) Concept conflict: Rather than always presenting the mostly agreed-upon concept or idea, flip it. This compels students to explore and reason for the conflicting idea, challenging their thinking and making them question their own thoughts or beliefs.

Examples:

- Geography: Climate change has nothing to do with humans.

- History: Bomber Harris was wrong to bomb Dresden.

- RE: The theory of evolution is true.

- Science: Cloning holds the future for mankind.

- English: In *Of Mice and Men*, George was right to kill Lennie.

4) Praise curiosity: If you want your students to do more of something, then catch them doing it and praise them for it. Whenever a student asks a question to further their learning and enhance their understanding of the subject, praise them for it and make a deal of it. That way the class learns that asking questions is a good thing and you create an atmosphere for questions.

5) Fill in the gaps: This challenge involves giving pairs of students two pictures: one from the start of the story, process, idea or experiment and one from the end. The challenge for the students is to work out the missing connections that link the images together. You could use a piece of text or parts of a flow chart or even text messages.

6) More questions than answers: Provide students with a photograph or image and challenge them to create questions generated from the stimuli.

7) Teacher vocabulary: Your words are powerful and they alone can empower students to take risks and give them the confidence to go to the edge of their comfort zone. Ask 'what do *you* think' questions: The answers to the questions we ask students are often derived from the theory, concept or ideas that we have been teaching them. For a different approach to the same content, instead ask them to consider what they would do in the same situation or what their own personal view is about a scenario.

The following question stems and phrases can be used to help to develop those traits. Give them a go and see how your students react.

- What's your opinion?

- Why do you think . . .?

- What would be the opposite view to that?

- What do you think will happen when . . .?

8) Hold back: Don't give the students all the information, ask them to fill in the gaps or to consider what they need to do. Provide them with the answer later, after they have investigated the problem or issue themselves.

For example, if you are teaching a science experiment, rather than having all the equipment and apparatus laid out ready for the students to use, alternatively start by asking them: 'What equipment do you think we could use to test the energy of a peanut?' This engages the student on a new level so instead of the students robotically collecting and using the equipment, they are now challenged to try and test other equipment. One group could be a control group using the 'correct' equipment. It may just be the spark that creativity and inspiration need to get students thinking deeper. Rather than give students solutions to problems, ask them to design or come up with their own ideas.

- Geography: Design an earthquake-proof building.

- Music: Select what instruments you may need to produce a piece of 'scary' music.

- D and T: What equipment will you need to make your bird box?

- History: Design your own Roman town.

Asking the students to attempt to answer the very questions that have tested the leading figures in your subject is a great way to engage them with the subject. Then you can share how others have tried to answer the same questions and solve problems, and the students discover how others have been successful.

9) What great questions have you asked today? Another concept to consider is to change the mindset towards learning. Instead of asking, 'What have you learned today?', try asking 'What great questions did you ask today?' By raising the profile of asking questions and being curious it should help to create a culture that is accepting and promotes questioning.

10) When you first introduce a topic, start by giving the students a quick overview of the topic. This could be an introductory movie clip or a series of pictures to prompt discussion. Give them enough information to make them curious, without answering a lot of the bigger questions they may have. Then ask the students to jot their questions onto a sticky note and to stick them on a wall. You can then refer to these questions as you cover the topic in the coming weeks or lessons, taking them off the wall as you answer them. This is an engaging activity for the students as they love to have their questions answered and taken off the wall.

## Creating creativity in the classroom

This can be a difficult concept to grasp: How can you make somebody creative? Especially since so many people seem to acknowledge that they are 'not very creative' or say that they 'never have any good ideas'. It's true you cannot just make somebody creative, but what you can do is create an environment and create the opportunity for creativity to grow.

## Devices to encourage creativity

1) **Chalk it**: We used to use it as children, yet as we grow we forget the enjoyment and creativity we had with just some simple chalk. Take your students outside to the playground or to vacant wall and let them go. With a bit of thought, you can easily come up with some ideas to get students designing or mapping out aspects of your subject. I get my students to design their own city. One group of students is in charge of transport links; another group, types of housing; another, entertainment facilities. They all enjoy the activity and, once finished, stand back and admire the work. It can be truly impressive. It is also a useful revision exercise: Ask them to condense information into a flow chart on a wall or sketch out key diagrams or pictures.

2) **Active Learning Exercises:** Every so often, or once or twice per term, engage your students with an Active Learning Exercise. This involves the following format:

   a) Think-pair-share: Students are given a differentiated open ended questions and they have a fixed amount of time to develop a presentation to answer the question. Each pair or group is then given one of the following resources that they have to use in order to present their answer.

   - A laptop/tablet

   - Felt tip and card

   - A roll of wall paper and pens

   - A box containing a mixture of craft resources

   - A box of chalk

   - A box containing a mixture of percussion instruments

   b) Then, using only the resources they have been given, they have to present their own informative presentation to display the answer to their particular question and answer any questions based on their work.

   c) Quiz: Once all pairs/groups have presented, organise a short quiz to test their recall and consolidation of the information they have been presented with.

   d) Assessment: After the quiz and debrief with the answers, the students have a written assessment based on the content of the lesson. This is the opportunity for the students to apply what they have learned.

3) When marking and offering feedback, consider setting targets specifically aimed at developing creativity in your classroom. Targets to help develop creativity:

- Take risks with your work by thinking, 'What would the best work include?'

- Try to include detail in your work from sources you haven't used before (for example: newspaper articles or radio broadcasts).

- Think up original ways to present your work and create revision materials.

- When answering questions, consider the alternative viewpoint to your argument.

- Practise developing links between different aspects of the topic; draw a series of pictures linking them together.

4) **Creative software**: If you want to get truly creative, then you must embrace technology. I realise schools can be at very different levels of funding and assistance and thus their spending may not reach the latest technological device for every student. However, there are a number of ways to make just a little bit of technology go a long way.

- Many schools now have handheld digital cameras or the like that can be used to film. Give these to students and let them get creative. Get them making movies, news reports, Vlogs and video diaries of your subject.

- Let students use smartphones in lessons to research the topic you are studying or to answer those great bizarre questions the students have that you cannot answer.

- Let students make their own selfie photo dairy whilst completing their homework. Or get then creating selfie stories to describe an aspect of the course.

- Use 'Socrative' (http://www.socrative.com) to monitor student responses to questions. It is an online application that allows teachers to assess students' responses using their phones.

- There is ever-increasing software and apps that allow you to share the content of one tablet with the rest of the class. A little bit of research and you can be using the school iPad in lessons to revolutionise your teaching practice.

- Ask students to create their own infographics using readily available software online. Infographics aim to condense a lot of information down into a number of key points with interesting and imaginative images and graphics to support understanding. These can then be pinned onto the school website or subject-specific web page to support other students.

I hope that you recognise that the majority of teaching ideas in this book are aimed to support creativity and create curiosity. Because through creativity and curiosity we generate enthusiasm and inspire greatness, and if we can get students enthused and inspired, they will learn for themselves.

**How to create a culture of creativity and curiosity, in a nutshell**

- It is important not to neglect creativity and curiosity at the expense of content.

- Creativity and curiosity are the very things that make students want to come to school.

- Creative lessons can often appear on the surface as 'fun' lessons lacking real purpose. Don't underestimate the thinking that is going on at a deeper level; it's a valuable time to let students discover and explore.

- Give students the opportunity to be creative and curious and they will reward you for it through increased engagement and improved achievement.

**Figure 14.1** How to create a culture of creativity and curiosity, in a nutshell

# 15

# Homework

There are few things that create a collective groan in the staffroom like the mention of homework. It has been an issue throughout my teaching career. The main debates seem to surround the following issues:

- Is it worthwhile setting at all?

- Is it worthwhile setting homework if only half the class completes it?

- The time used and effort made chasing up and collecting homework from those students who have failed to meet the deadline.

- How homework meets the expectations of parents.

- Should all the students get the same homework?

- How much should teachers set?

Having looked at some issues from the teacher's point of view, now let's consider the students. How do they feel about homework? Obviously, all schools are different but, in my experience, many students find homework boring and do not place it in very high regard. So why is that? The answer lies with us as teachers. If we do not place it in high regard, and merely see it as an 'add on' to a lesson, then students will treat it as such. It should be planned carefully, rather than quickly thrown together as the class is packing away. At this point, I would ask you to consider the following questions:

Is your homework differentiated to meet the needs of the different groups of students in your class? Is it engaging and challenging or just another poster? Do you mark it and offer feedback? Is it relevant? Does it link to previous or future lessons?

The reality is that if it is an afterthought for teachers then it is likely to be an afterthought for students. I do not mean to preach on this topic; I, along with many staff, feel the burden of setting and marking homework. But by giving homework some careful consideration and planning, it can be an incredibly useful device to improve student performance and help you develop resources, as well as help to develop an efficient and effective learning habit.

The merits of homework have been debated in educational circles for many years, with various papers discussing a range of topics, from its impact on mental health to the amount of homework time expected of seven-year-olds. Personally, I cannot see how an appropriate amount of homework can be detrimental to a student. I suppose the next question is, 'What is an appropriate amount?' Well, this is for you to decide, but be realistic. In fact, asking the students what they consider realistic will go some way toward giving you an answer. This may seem a strange approach to some, and I do not ask all my classes, but on the whole I have been impressed with the student responses. We arrive at a compromise on both number of challenges and also the deadlines. This discussion often leads to more students 'buying in' to the homework because it was a mutually agreed-upon task and deadline. I should also point out that, for me, it's all about the quality rather than the quantity. I do not need pages and pages of copied-and-pasted notes from the internet; what I'd prefer is three paragraphs of insightful and concise note taking. I believe that homework serves a range of purposes:

- Develops autonomy and independent study skills.

- Supports recall.

- Consolidates exiting learning.

- Develops research skills.

- Supports creativity.

- Stimulates reflection on previous work.

- Supports application of knowledge and understanding.

- Develops time management skills.

- Provides an opportunity to practise.

- Provides an opportunity to action feedback.

## How to design homework that has an impact

Quality homework is the result of quality planning; a bit of time invested at the start can save you heaps of time in the long run. Planning can provide a programme of challenges that you can refer to time and again, and it produces creative and impressive work that not only improves student performance, but also creates work you can use as a resource or model in the future. As mentioned earlier, student apathy towards homework stems from a number of issues, and therefore planning gives us the opportunity to tackle these problems so that we receive higher quality work from more and more students, time and time again. The key to quality homework is to deliver activities that are: challenging for all, engaging and motivating, relevant to the students and offering students independence and ownership. If you can tick these boxes, then I am confident that homework quality and engagement will increase.

# Take away homework

Whoever first came up with this idea is a genius! When I first came across the idea, I was blown away by its simplicity to implement – and later by the quality of work it would go on to produce. It takes some work to put in place, but once incorporated into your lessons, it can have a huge impact on improving student performance.

It works as follows: Students pick from the menu of activities, thus providing autonomy and independence, and because the students chose the challenges, they take ownership of their learning and this increases engagement and motivation. The fact that students get the opportunity to pick what they do has a huge impact on their engagement and motivation. In my experience, students enjoy looking through the menu and discussing with their partners what they are thinking of choosing, sharing ideas and enthusing about how they will deliver the various challenges.

The challenges are differentiated, with different components of the menu offering different levels of challenge for all students. The tasks can be clearly linked to previous or future lessons.

The benefit for teachers is that the menu can be topic specific or it can be a generic set of challenges that can be applied to a number of classes. The example in Table 15.1 is a generic takeaway homework grid that can be applied to a number of subjects. To make it more subject or topic specific, simply replace or introduce more challenges tailored to suit the subject or your students' needs.

The advantage of the generic menu is that it reduces work load. Instead of having to continually produce a new take away homework menu, it can be used throughout the year. I must stress that this is not the only homework template I use; it would become boring for the students and they would soon be disengaged. I use a range of approaches throughout the term and year to keep things interesting and fresh. One week I may set a take away homework challenge, the next week a project-based approach. It's a case of tapping into the needs of your students and tuning in to how they are progressing. They may enjoy the take away homework tasks (in which case, continue with them) or they may need a project to enable them to get to grips with a particularly difficult aspect of the course.

Take away homework is beneficial because the challenges help students to recall, consolidate and apply the learning. In the previous chapter, I wrote about the need for students to consolidate their learning. If the students are to remember what we have taught them, they must transfer that knowledge or skill to their long term memory; thus homework challenges can help to develop these skills and consolidate what students have learned in previous lessons or during the topic.

The activities have different levels of challenge to them, and this allows you the opportunity to differentiate the activities for the students. For example, you may set high ability students the challenge of completing one 'starter' and two 'mains' whilst setting low ability students two 'starters' and one 'sweet'. You may just want each student to select two challenges from each category on the menu to complete. The challenges can be set over a number of lessons or weeks, giving students flexibility and the choice of when they work on the tasks; they develop time management skills in the process. You may ask students to complete one challenge and then bring it to the lesson to be marked before setting another challenge. You may ask for the students to complete six challenges over the next six weeks, two from each category. The menu gives you as the teacher a great flexibility to choose what challenges you set, and these can be suited to meet the needs of individual students or groups of students.

The fact that you have devoted the time to produce such a resources emphasises the importance of homework to your students. Instead of homework being an after-thought, it now becomes an integral part of the students' learning, especially if you emphasise the importance of the challenges to improve their consolidation of knowledge and ultimately exam performance. It may be necessary for students to complete a specific challenge for a future lesson. In the past, I have insisted that students pick one specific challenge that results in them producing a resource that will be used in a future lesson, thus making it relevant and useful for the student. Therefore, it is not a throwaway task, but something they can see as useful to their own learning and development within your subject.

The work that students deliver can often go beyond all expectations. Many times I have been impressed by what the students have produced with open ended challenges such as 'produce a movie' or 'create a model'. I am sure that they will inspire and impress you with what they can come up with. The benefit for us as teachers is that we can often use students' work as examples of good practice or use it as a learning resources in subsequent lessons.

If students are going to the effort of producing homework, then they deserve feedback. Consider the scenario from their viewpoint: They put their effort in at home working on a particular challenge, dedicating time to produce something that they are proud of, never to receive any recognition. How would you feel?

If you want them to do more of something, you have to catch them doing it and praise them for it. If they go to the effort of making a model or producing a short movie, and they receive no recognition for their effort, why would they ever want to go to that effort again? This does not mean that you have to necessarily mark every piece of homework; it just means that every piece of homework should be recognised. This can be done with peer assessment and class discussions. One approach I use is for students to open their books at their homework pages and arrange them on a back table. Then, as a class, we discuss which pieces of homework we consider to be the best, and why. Because students cannot see names on the fronts of books it creates a sense of anonymity; thus, students can be more frank with their feedback, which in my experience is far more positive. This work can then be copied and used as a model for other classes to refer to, if you so wish. In fact, I have used a number of student resources within lessons because their work is so outstanding.

**Table 15.1** Takeaway homework

| Starter | Main | Sweet |
|---|---|---|
| Create a poster summarising the main points of today's lesson. | Make a movie on the key ideas, concepts and/or processes of the topic we have been studying. | Write a poem or song inspired by one or all of the aspects of the topic we have been learning about. |
| Write three tweets to a friend explaining what you have learned in today's lesson. | Create a comic strip to explain what we have been learning about during this topic. | Write a newspaper article based on today's lesson. |
| Create a mind map linking the key ideas and concepts of today's lesson or the topic which we have been studying. | Design a flow chart or diagram to explain an idea, concept or process we have been learning about. | Design a word-search or crossword using the key terms of this topic. |
| Create a set of flash cards for the topic containing key words and their definitions. | Design a foldable to describe and explain a key idea concept or process we have been learning about during this topic. | Write ten challenge questions for your class mates to answer based on our current topic. |
| Design a board game based on the topic we are studying. | Create your own project work based on one key aspect of the topic. | Make your own revision poster based on the work we have covered this topic. |
| Write a postcard to a friend explaining what you have learned in today's lesson. | Create a set of pictures to summarise the topic. | Design a leaflet about what you have learned during this topic. |
| List eight points that you have learned during this topic and then prioritise them (number one being the most important thing and number eight the least). Write why number one is the most important. | Create your own mnemonic to remember a key idea, concept or process from this topic. | Develop your own 'mind palace' to remember eight key points from the topic. |
| Produce a piece of artwork or a 3D model to demonstrate your understanding of our current topic. | Write an exam style question and a mark scheme based on one aspect of our current topic. | Write a progress report for yourself, outlining what you are doing well and what you need to do to improve. |
| What do you know now that you didn't at the start of this topic? Write down six points. | Write ten multiple choice questions to test your class mates based on the topic we are studying. | Create an infographic on part or all of the topic we are studying. |

## Pot luck

This homework activity can be used to support your teaching and involves students actively participating within lessons.

- Start by dividing your topic up into a number of key concepts, ideas or questions.

- Write these on slips of paper and ask individuals or groups of students to pick a slip from the hat.

- The students then either work individually or in groups to produce a presentation based on their chosen concept.

- The topic areas will be linked to lessons you are teaching; therefore, you can use students' work to complement what you will be teaching in the lesson. Students can then present their work during an interval in the lesson.

- Students or groups of students are given specific deadlines to tie in to your lesson planning. Therefore, some students may have a tight deadline of next lesson whereas other students may have several weeks to produce their presentations.

## Hints

1) The questions I write for the students to research and answer are the same learning questions I use in my lessons; thus, they dovetail perfectly and I know that the content will support what I will be teaching.

2) The more detail, the better. If you want quality work, be specific on what content you are after.

3) Inspire your students to produce 'outstanding' work, show them model work from previous classes and allow them flexibility on how they will complete the challenge. Depending upon your class, you may need to set a minimum standard (for example, a minimum of six slides).

## Flipped learning

This was first discussed in Chapter 9, 'Moving away from modelling'. As mentioned, the premise is to flip the more traditional approach to classwork and homework. The students learn the content and lower order knowledge at home via online lectures, tutorials, video clips or reading and then during the lesson this knowledge is discussed and synthesised (higher order skills).

How it works:

1) Introduce students to the idea of 'flipped learning'. It is important to tell the students why they are doing it and to talk them through the process. Explain what is expected from them and how they are being given ownership of their own learning. This helps students buy into the idea.

2) Resources: You need to provide the resources for students to engage with at home or outside of the classroom. The main resource used in flipped learning is online video clips. These can be made be yourself, by the students or gathered online from

websites. There are a wealth of short useful videos that can be found on websites such as BBC Bytesize, TED-ED, Khan Academy or YouTube. This content will then form the basis of your lesson.

I am aware that not all students have access to the internet or they may be absent from the lesson. The best remedy for this is either for students to use the school's resources at breaks, lunchtimes or the end of school, or to have a computer in your classroom so students are able to watch the relevant clip if they have missed it whilst the other students continue with the lesson.

You may need to explain to students how to watch video clips. Rather than sit passively watching, they can make notes on the clip or create a storyboard. They may need to rewind at certain points to watch again a key idea or concept.

Although video clips are often the main medium for information, it is important to offer a variety of resources; alternatives may be a radio broadcast, a podcast, a newspaper article or a journal.

3) Active learning: Students arrive at your lesson having engaged with the resources and ready to apply what they have learned.

4) Open ended questions/discussion: You may want to begin the lesson discussing the resources the students have been using at home; this may be a think, pair, share activity or a structured debate on the key points.

5) Challenge: This section of the lesson consists of a challenge or a number of challenges you may want your students to complete based on their learning. For example, read through a conflicting argument to the homework resource, or produce a presentation based on the homework resources. Whatever the challenge, the idea is that it is a higher level task than that set for homework.

6) Consolidation: To consolidate the learning, perhaps conduct a ten-question quiz.

7) Application: Students apply what they have learned by completing an exam paper question or a short test.

## How to motivate students to complete homework consistently

An issue you may face with homework is getting all students to participate and complete it. There may be a number of reasons for this that you may discuss with individual students. It could be that home life is not conducive to homework. They may not have a desk at home or have access to a computer, for example. If this is the case, hopefully your school can run a study club or homework club that will help to mitigate against these issues. However, a common reason for failure to complete homework to a desired standard is because a student could not be bothered. So aside from making the homework as interesting and engaging as possible, how else can we motivate students?

Below is a list of points I ask my students to write down and read before they begin any homework or when they look in their book/folder. It is an intrinsic motivation tool aimed at developing the study habit.

## Reasons to do my homework and study now!

- This could be the difference between a pass and a fail.

- This is a small step to achieving all I dream of.

- I can be proud of what I have achieved and others will be proud of me.

- Think how good I will feel once I have finished my work well.

- Nothing worth having is easily obtained; I am going to have to work hard for it.

- Turn off the mobile, concentrate and get on with it!

- What are you waiting for?

Another approach is to involve them in the homework planning process. Rather than you designing all the homework challenges, ask them what homework they would like to do. Involving the students and valuing their input increases their uptake with the challenges, and they may come up with imaginative homework ideas you had not considered. Of course, not all suggestions may be appropriate; however, their ideas can guide you to developing challenges that will match their curiosity and engage them to complete the work set.

## Dialogue to support: Homework

'Planners out, write down your homework, don't put them away until I have checked that it is written down, this way we can have no excuses for forgetting to do it.'

'What do you think is a fair deadline date?'

'How many challenges do you think you could complete?'

'Are we all clear on what we have to do? Susan, repeat back to me what you have to do for your homework.'

'How many challenges do you have to complete?'

'When is the deadline for this homework?'

'If you have any questions, queries or concerns about your homework, see me before the deadline date.'

**Homework, in a nutshell**

- Homework should be set to reflect, recall, consolidate, apply or inform learning.

- Planning appropriate homework challenges will increase the engagement from students.

- Offering choice of homework challenges aids student differentiation as well as providing students with independence, flexibility and autonomy.

- Use students' homework as teaching resources, whether that be as models of good practice or as stand-alone resources for others to use.

**Figure 15.1**   Homework, in a nutshell

# 16

# Plenaries

The aim of a plenary should be closely linked to the aims suggested in Chapter 13 regarding how to get students to remember what you teach them. Both approaches are associated with students reflecting on what they have learned and consolidating their learning into their long term memory. The aim of an effective plenary should be to establish links; it is these links and the connection that the student makes that help to consolidate the learning into memory so it can be stored and accessed at a later date.

When you started teaching, what country you teach in and which training sessions you have attended will all influence your approach to plenaries. When I first started teaching, a two-minute question and answer session as the students were packing away was ample. I'm afraid that doesn't cut it anymore, and neither should it. No wonder the students would come into the next lesson not having a clue what we did the previous lesson. The same rules apply to plenaries that apply to memory techniques: the more colourful, dramatic, outrageous and funny you can make the plenary, the more likely it is that the students will remember what you taught them.

As with starters, I have a PowerPoint presentation of the following plenaries. I can then tailor or amend each slide as necessary, and the students have learned the habit of knowing how to approach each of the challenges. The examples below are ten of my favourite and most commonly used plenaries, which have the greatest impact on the students' progress. They are the challenges that students genuinely enjoy, and this enjoyment translates into consolidation and helps students to recall and review their learning.

1) **What am I thinking of?** For this challenge, students are allowed to ask six questions based on the lesson before they have to guess what I am thinking. This activity works well because, in order for the students to create questions and guess the answers, they must have a degree of recall. I don't mind if students look back in the books or look at their notes, but for increased challenge ask the students to shut their books before you start. To make this more dramatic, you could wear a silly hat, your 'telepathy hat', and to make the scene more entertaining I sometimes follow up the correct answer

by asking the student a few questions to see if we truly have a telepathic link. I write down the answers to the following questions and then reveal them later.

'I'm thinking of a country beginning with D. What is it?'

'Which vegetable am I thinking of?'

'Which animal am I thinking of?'

You would be surprised by the number of students who reply with *Denmark, carrot* and *elephant*. Of course you do not have to ask just one question; come up with a number of questions or ask students to wear the 'telepathy hat'.

2) **Word association:** Students are asked to create their own word association poster. This may be in a format similar to a 'wordle' or as a circular diagram with each word linked to the next. Students may use larger words to signify their importance to the topic. This can be added to each lesson so that at the end of a unit of work, the students have a comprehensive list of linked words all associated with the topic that they can use to revise from or to support recall.

3) **I have progressed by . . .** This is a useful technique requiring the students to reflect on their own learning. You may need to set clear expectations, depending on your class (for example: 'List six key points' or 'Write ten lines to explain what you have learned and how you have progressed'). This can then be followed up by asking them to write: 'What Went Well' (WWW) and 'Even Better If' (EBI). I then ask students to share their thoughts with the class: It is useful for students to hear what others have learned because it triggers recall for them, and it is also useful for the teacher as it may highlight any misconceptions or gaps in learning, which can be addressed next lesson.

4) **Speed dating:** For this activity, students may need to arrange their desks so that they can move around the room and also sit opposite to one another. I find a horseshoe arrangement works best with students sitting on the outside and inside of the desks, or you may clear away the desks and just have two circles of students sitting opposite. Sitting opposite each other, students have two minutes to discuss what they have learned during the lesson. Then once the time is up, I ask the inner circle of students to move around one place so everyone is now talking to someone else.

This is a fantastic way to get students to talk about their learning and, in my experience, because the time allowed is so short, they are rarely off task. Depending on your class, you may want to shorten the time or lengthen it, but I find an online timer projected onto the board works well so that the students can see how much time is remaining.

If you feel the class may lack confidence in such an activity, you can give the students time to produce a learning resource that they can use when explaining what they have learned. I always enjoy this challenge; it is a great way to see all students on task and actively engaging in discussion. I even put on a bit of Barry White to really set the mood!

5) **Tweets, texts and emojis:** These are fun ways to engage students whilst they are reviewing the lesson. Students must either write a tweet of 140 characters or fewer to sum up what they have learned during the lesson or compose a text to a friend. I allow them to use text language as this increases student engagement and also challenges them to think about how they can transfer what they have learned to another medium. Students can summarise the lesson or piece of text they have been using by creating a series of emojis to represent what they have learned. This is a great way to get the students to make connections and transfer information whilst consolidating what they have learned. I have created my own templates simply by using images off the internet of a Twitter feed and a picture of a mobile phone. Students can then either pass these around the class to read each other's comments or stick them in their book for me to review. They also aid recall at the start of the next lesson if you ask students to review what they wrote.

6) **Slaps:** This activity works best with smaller class sizes, although it has been successful with thirty students. This is how it works:

- All the students sit around the tables in the centre of the room.

- The students then put their out-stretched hands on the table.

- Then students place their hands underneath and alongside their neighbours hand.

- Once all students' hands are on the table and next to each other, one student begins by slapping his hand on the table.

- The next hand to the right then follows suit.

- The aim is to make the slaps fast and continuous until they have been all around the table.

- If a student is too slow or too early, then he/she has to answer a question from the teacher.

- Once the students get the hang of this, you can introduce new rules.

- Two slaps on the table reverses the direction.

- Three slaps on the table skips a hand in the same direction.

My students love this activity and they are all so engaged and enthusiastic. The questions you ask as a teacher could be low level review questions or higher level questions that could be discussed around the table. The same rules apply as from my chapter on questioning. If a student does not know the answer I ask somebody else and then go back to ask the original student to repeat what he/she has just heard.

7) **Mime or picture:** For this challenge, I ask all students to jot down on a piece of paper key words or phrases from either the lesson or the topic we have been studying. Then, having collected all the pieces of paper in a hat, students must come to the front of the class and either mime the key word or draw a picture of it on the board for the other students to guess. You could divide the class into teams if you want to increase the level of competition or simply ask students to tally how many they guess correctly. This is a great way to consolidate learning, and the resources the students produce can be used again with another class or kept to be used again in a future lesson.

8) **Who/what am I?** This activity involves using those key words or phrases that the students may have produced for mime/picture. With the students either sitting or standing in a circle, the teacher gives each student a slip of paper that they are unable to see, and sticks it to the student's forehead. Then, in turn, the student directs questions to the group, attempting to guess what is written on the piece of paper on the student's forehead. Since this challenge involves subject-specific terms or phrases, it requires that the students have a good knowledge and understanding of the subject. It also allows you as the teacher to spot gaps in the students' learning or any misunderstandings or misconceptions.

9) **Game of Thrones**: For this challenge, students have to answer questions and move seats or 'thrones'. You begin by asking a question to a pair of students sat next to each other, and whoever says the answer first wins. I then let the winner sit in my swivel chair to move to the next contestant at the next table. The aim is to move to as many tables as possible before losing; whoever gets the question right first gets to sit in the throne. Rather than me having to come up with a series of questions, prior to this activity I ask the students to write down three questions they think could test the class. I then collect these in and use these for the game.

10) **Key question carousel:** This activity involves the groups of students sharing ideas to answer a key question related to their learning. Each group is given either the same question or different questions related to the lesson. Then students discuss and share ideas to plan and write a model answer to the question. After an allotted time, the students move around the room to either add to another group's answer or complete another task (for example, to storyboard the original answer).

**Example:**

Challenge 1: The group plans and writes a model answer to the key question.

Challenge 2: Students add to or improve the original response to the question.

Challenge 3: Students read through the answer and highlight eight key points from the answer, including key words and connectives.

Challenge 4: Students storyboard six key points from the answer.

Challenge 5: Students condense the text into 20 words.

After the students have completed all the challenges and read the other groups' work, they return to their original work, read through the improvement and reflect on the responses. You may want them to amend their original answer or take a photograph on their phone of the work and produce a revision resource for their homework.

**Plenaries, in a nutshell**

- The key aim of a plenary is to consolidate or apply what the students have been learning.

- You want it to serve as a book end to the lesson.

- Link the plenary to the learning question.

- Ask students to reflect on what they have learned by completing: 'I have progressed by . . .'

- Focus your plenary by asking yourself, 'What is the most important thing I want them to take away from this lesson?'

**Figure 16.1**   Plenaries, in a nutshell

# 17

# Time management

## Habits and hacks to help you become more efficient in the workplace

There can be little argument that the workload within the teaching profession has increased. With increasing workloads come increasing expectations, and these can result in increased levels of stress. It is therefore unsurprising that teaching often appears in the 'top five most stressful jobs' lists. There are a number of contributing factors to stress within the job, but one of the main issues is the feeling that there is not enough time to complete all the tasks to a desired standard. It is unsurprising that with the demands placed on us from students, senior leaders, colleagues and parents, we all feel time pressures. That's not even including life outside of school: family, friends and trying to find some time for ourselves. In this chapter, I outline habits that I have developed that have enabled me to cope with these pressures and cultivate a feeling of accomplishment.

I appreciate that time is a precious resource; however, don't make lack of time an excuse for not getting things done. Parkinson's Law states: Work expands to fill the time allotted to it. If you have three weeks to write a set of reports, then it will likely take three weeks; however, if we only have one day to complete them, we likely can do it in one day. There is another saying in business: 'If you want something done, ask a busy person.' Become that busy person. Be action oriented. Don't sit about waiting for things to happen to you; get going; get active. As Richard Branson says, 'screw it – let's do it.' For many of us, our contracted working day is seven hours – for example, 8:30–3:30. I know that we all work many more hours than this, but on a daily basis that leaves us with approximately another 6–7 hours – almost another working day. So how are you spending that time? I pass no judgement on this; it is just a question for you to think about. Could you spend that time more wisely? I know I could.

## Time management habits

Learn to love lists: Get into the habit of making lists. I know many people hate working from a list; others admit to writing lists but never completing anything off them. For me, making lists is the number one habit that allows me to work most efficiently. It allows me to prioritise my tasks, gives me clarity on what needs to be accomplished and ensures I don't forget any important duties. I have two lists I use: one for the week and a daily list of things to do. This is how to works:

a) Write down all the things you have to accomplish in the week. This may include both work and home life. Consult calendars or newsletters to make sure you do not miss any important dates and to see what is coming up in the next few weeks. Having made the weekly list of things to do, divide them up into daily tasks.

b) Having made this list, prioritise the tasks. Ask yourself the following questions:

'What is my most important task?'

'If I could only complete one thing off this list, what would it be?'

'What is the most valuable use of my time?'

You should find that this crystallises your top task. Then put a number '1' next to this task, and work your way down the list, numbering items in order of importance.

c) Get to work on number one. You may need to break your number one tasks down further, so write down all the steps necessary to complete your top challenge, and then again prioritise these sub tasks. These will formulate your daily duties and give you clarity on what you need to accomplish.

d) Do it now. Get going and just do it. If you can develop this one characteristic, it alone will triple your productivity. Become action oriented, and work on those tasks that are going to give you the greatest benefit. Of course, there are times when we all have to do those jobs we dislike, but if it needs doing then it needs doing. Moaning about it or complaining will not change the situation, so accept it, deal with it and move on.

e) It is vital that you stick to your list of priorities. Many people get caught up with the easy menial tasks and lose sight of the vital few challenges that it is imperative to complete.

It is often the case that the important tasks are the ones you would like to put off: that phone call to a parent or the pile of books yet to be marked. But the books are not going to go away and the parent will still be waiting. It is useful to consider the consequences of uncompleted tasks to help motivate yourself to accomplish them. For example, if the books go unmarked, then the students will suffer because they require feedback on how to improve their work. Add into this that your head of department or senior managers will not be impressed with books going unmarked for several weeks. The parent you need to ring will only become more frustrated and annoyed by the lack of response, which may escalate the issue you need to discuss. In addition to the third parties involved, consider how you will be feeling. Putting off uncomfortable but necessary tasks can create anxiety. Knowing that you still haven't rung the parent will make you fear the worst, building the problem up in your mind. Far better to get it over with so you can concentrate on other important tasks.

f) Concentration: Develop the habit of completing tasks. Start with your most important task and stick with it until it is complete. Once you have completed it, reward yourself. This may be a cup of tea or watching an episode of your favourite TV show. This task reward system will help you develop will power and motivation; the more you complete tasks, the easier it becomes to do it time and time again.

g) Set yourself deadlines to complete tasks. If you can, when tasks come along complete them as soon as possible. Develop a sense of urgency so challenges don't linger on for days or weeks. Parkinson's Law states: Work expands to fill the time allotted to it. Give yourself one week to write the report instead of three, and this frees up more time for you to accomplish other tasks.

h) Allot certain time to certain tasks: Try to batch tasks together. For example, set time aside at the end of the day to make all your phone calls, or respond to e-mails during lunchtime and only lunchtime. Don't fall into the trap of feeling like you need to respond to e-mails straight away. In many cases, the majority of e-mails do not need to be actioned, and if they are vitally important nine times out of ten the person will contact you directly or e-mail you again.

## Time management hacks: Quick wins to help you manage your time efficiently

1) Ask direct questions: We are often asked to complete tasks by senior leaders, heads of department/faculty and work colleagues. One way to avoid misspent time and effort is to ask one or more of the following questions to get straight to the point and the heart of the matter.

    a) 'What is it that you specifically want?'

    b) 'My understanding of this is . . . is that correct?'

    c) 'What results are you expecting?'

    d) 'When are you expecting this to be completed by?'

    e) 'Can you give me an example of what it is you are after?'

    f) 'Can you clarify . . .?'

These questions should help you understand what you are required to do and ensure that you are both clear on the expected outcome.

2) Marking 1: When you are collecting in books to be marked, have the students open their books to the first pages that you need to mark. This task alone can save you valuable minutes (rather than having to wade through pages to find the appropriate starting point time and time again).

3) Marking 2: I would not suggest this become a regular practice, but marking the students work whilst you are teaching them can provide a valuable opportunity to discuss the students' work with them whilst also allowing you to complete your marking. It provides the opportunity to discuss misconceptions, student progress and what they can do to improve their work. You could ask students to record the conversation in their book as 'verbal feedback' so they have something in their books that they can refer back to.

4) Calendar deadlines: Make sure you always hit deadlines by writing them down. I photocopy, enlarge and highlight the school calendar, which I then stick on my wall so I am always aware of what important dates are coming up. Having the calendar on a wall that I see daily means that there are no surprises, and I can organise my time around those key dates.

5) Delegate to students: Give students responsibility; many of them thrive off it. Develop the role of lead learner to support other students, freeing you up to work with individuals or groups. Rather than you always producing the teaching resources, delegate this task to the students. It may be the case that they are more creative and also produce resources pitched at just the right level for your students. For example: If you are looking to use pictures for a back to back drawing challenge, instead of you having to troll through the internet to find appropriate pictures, set it as part of a homework challenge. Be specific in your instruction on what you are expecting, and then these images can be collected in, mixed up and redistributed for the activity. Challenge them to produce their own revision resource on the topic you have been learning and then you can use the best resources with another class. There are always opportunities to challenge students to be creative, and these resources can be shared as good practice and modelled.

6) Meetings: Meetings can be a huge waste of time if they are not managed well. Make sure the meeting has a clear purpose. It you are leading the meeting, start by saying 'The purpose of this meeting is . . .' and this way everybody is clear why they are there. If you are not leading the meeting, ask 'What is the purpose of this meeting?' This question will help to clarify the expectations and outcomes of the meeting.

7) Don't get distracted: You must give yourself a fighting chance to get things done. So to do this, give yourself time free from distraction; create situations and environments that allow you to concentrate on completing tasks. I like to get into work very early because I know there is nobody around to distract me, chat to me, ask me questions

or take me away from my top priorities that will give me the largest benefit. I start the day with my most important task because I know I have the environment in which to accomplish that challenge; once it is complete, it gives me a sense of achievement that then motivates me to complete my other tasks throughout the day. During this time, I do not look at e-mails, I always have my phone off and I shut my door. It is my time to achieve. Create your own distraction-free environment. Whether this is at work or home, you need time to get your list of tasks completed. Shut the door, put your phone away and concentrate. Concentrating on just one task will shorten the time it takes to complete it.

8) Marginal gains: When it comes to time management, every second counts. Think about how you spend your time during the day and consider ways you can reduce wasted time. For example, could you have a kettle in your room that would save you having to trudge to the staffroom and getting distracted in idle conversation that wastes all of your break-time? Make sandwiches for your lunch so you are not stuck in long queues and park closer to the school entrance to speed up your day. All these saved seconds and minutes add up and create those marginal gains that allow you to accomplish more. I realise that working out how you can save seconds and minutes may appear obsessive, but is it obsessive or is it good time management?

9) Synergy: This is the interaction of elements that, when combined, produce a total effect that is greater than the sum of all the individual elements. Learn from other colleagues and collaborate to create a better way. Time can be saved by simply asking a colleague how he/she does things and carries out procedures. These professional conversations may even spark a new idea to make the procedure more efficient, thus creating synergy. When I start teaching a new class, I always ask colleagues if they see any potential problems or issues with my seating plan; this can save a lot of frustration and time rearranging students and dealing with poor behaviour. Share ideas on paper work: How do different departments write reports, compose important letters or mark books? All these interactions can be hugely beneficial; don't suffer in silence, getting more and more frustrated. Learn from others.

10) Sharpen the saw: In his book *The Seven Habits of Highly Effective People* (2004), Stephen Covey refers to sharpening the saw: Take some time to refresh and recharge (sharpen the saw) so you can become efficient and productive again. Time for yourself is a key dimension to overall time management. If you persist with tasks when you are tired or you are not concentrating, then this can often result in you making mistakes, and a task that should have taken 30 minutes has now stretched out to over 2 hours. I once worked with a colleague who would often announce to the staffroom how she had been working to the early hours of the morning and how she had been waking before dawn so she could complete all her work. Rather than be impressed with her commitment, I would rather reflect that she must have been incredibly

inefficient with her time. There are no 'prizes' for the number of hours worked, only for the impact and outcome of those hours.

If you are to remain on top of your game, then you must take time to refresh and recharge. My father always says, 'work hard, play hard'. So yes, work to the best of your ability – and also take time to do those things you enjoy. Fatigue is a growing problem within the profession, with drop-out rates of teachers increasing year on year. You must be able to separate work from home.

The merits of physical exercise are well documented to help restore energy levels and release endorphins that make you feel happy, so any regular exercise – whether that be swimming, jogging or yoga – all helps you to re-energise. Do not make the excuse that you are too busy working to be able to exercise. We can all find a bit of time to exercise; in addition, the very act will give you more energy, allowing you to work more efficiently.

Spending time with family and friends, reading a book or just having some time by yourself may all help to restore your well-being. Indulge in activities that make you happy; it may help to give you a better perspective on your work and reassure you that teaching is not the be-all and end-all. Sometimes the best thing to do when you come home from work is just to go to bed as early as possible – a good night's sleep may be the best use of your time if it leaves you feeling ready to get up and get going on the day ahead.

> **Time management, in a nutshell**
>
> - Make lists and prioritise your tasks.
> - Start with your highest priority first.
> - Stick with it until it is complete.
> - Ask yourself: Is this the best use of my time?
> - Learn from others: Ask others how they complete specific tasks.
> - Create distraction-free environments.
> - Make time for yourself.

**Figure 17.1** Time management, in a nutshell

# Bibliography

AQA (2016) 'Geography A (930) Specification'. Available: http://www.aqa.org.uk/subjects/geography/gcse/geography-a-9030

Dr Edward Banfield (1970) *The Un-heavenly City*. Little Brown and Co, London.

Geoff Barton (2012) *Don't Call it Literacy!* Routledge, Oxford.

Tony Buzan (2003) *Use Your Memory*. BBC Active, London.

Stephen Covey (2004) *The Seven Habits of Highly Effective People*. Simon & Schuster Ltd, London.

Charles Duhigg (2013) *The Power of Habit*. Random House Books, London.

Carol Dweck (2012) *Mindset: How You Can Fulfil Your Potential*. Robinson, London.

Carol Dweck (2014, November) 'The Power of Believing That You Can Improve'. TED Talk. Transcript and video available: https://www.ted.com/talks/carol_dweck_the_power_of_believing_that_you_can_improve/transcript?language=en

The Free Dictionary (2016) 'Habit'. Available: www.thefreedictionary.com

John Hattie (2011) *Visible Learning for Teachers*. Routledge, Oxford.

Peter Hook and Andy Vass (2011) *Behaviour Management Pocketbook*. Teachers Pocketbook, Alresford.

Lori D. Oczkus (2010) *Reciprocal Teaching at Work: Powerful Strategies and Lessons for Improving Reading Comprehension*. International Reading Association, Newark, DE.

Ken Robinson (2006, February) 'Do Schools Kill Creativity?' TED Talk. Transcript and video available: https://www.ted.com/talks/ken_robinson_says_schools_kill_creativity/transcript?language=en

Alistair Smith (1996) *Accelerated Learning in the Classroom*. Network Educational Press Ltd, Bristol.

Ian Smith (2007) *Sharing Learning Intentions*. Learning Unlimited, London.

Dinah Zike (2000) *Foldables: Handbook 3-D Graphic Organizers for Social Studies: Student and Teacher Support Resources*. Macmillan/McGraw-Hill, New York.

# Index